Cloud Memoir:

Selected Longer Poems

1987-2017

Christopher Buckley

STEPHEN F. AUSTIN STATE UNIVERSITY PRESS

Thanks to Richard Mathews and the University of Tampa Press for permission to reprint poems from *Rolling the Bones* and *White Shirt.*

Thanks to the University of Pittsburgh Press for permission to reprint "The Presocratic, Surfing, Breathing Cosmology Blues . . ." which appeared in *Star Journal: Selected Poems*, 2016, (c) the University of Pittsburgh Press.

Thanks to Tuck Schneider, friend of over 60 years, for the vintage postcard of Montecito, Santa Barbara, used for the cover.

For more information:
Stephen F. Austin State University Press
P.O. Box 13007 SFA Station
Nacogdoches, Texas 75962
sfapress@sfasu.edu
sfasu.edu/sfapress

Distributed by Texas A&M Consortium
tamupress.com

ISBN: 978-1-62288-212-0

First Edition

Preface

You reach a certain age . . . you talk to yourself more often . . . recently I've been asking myself what ever happened to my long poems? In a Selected Poems, published a couple years back, room was found for only one. And practically, you can't take up most of a reading with a long poem—you need to keep it moving, a little humor, a narrative handle for those unfamiliar with your work—keep folks who were kind enough to attend engaged/awake.

So a problem presented itself as I've often felt, however immodestly, that the longer poems often were the strongest work. A more or less symphonic structure—theme, variation, recapitulation—fits, it seems, my mind's habits, its speculative formations, its this/but that, its faith-and-doubt. Rarely did/do the grey cells and the music of experience organize themselves for me into expeditious dramatic or pithy movements. Alas. . . . Nevertheless, I've been content with the longer efforts over the years, the nostalgic, metaphysical, historical, and putative room to move they provide. My hope is that the more expansive strategies as I've worked with them are found worthy.

Inviting Philip Levine to read while I taught at various universities, living in Fresno for a number of years, I must have heard him read 25 times, probably more. Always, Phil gave powerful, gritty, inventive, electric, soul-making readings, counterpointed by his fantastic sense of humor between poems. But probably the most amazing reading I heard him give was at the Dodge Festival in New Jersey in 1996. The big tent there, the main venue, was packed. Phil read "A Walk With Tom Jefferson," a roughly 600 line poem. Pretty much unheard of—daring, risky to try and keep an audience engaged with a single poem for 40 or more minutes. Yet he did so—everyone following his history in Detroit to the larger "Biblical" history of people struggling on the planet. If you have a poem as large in scope, as poignant and compelling as "Tom Jefferson" it's possible. That leaves most of us out—not something I think I'd try. "Don't get any big ideas kid," I can still hear someone advising me back in my early 20s. . . . Still, Phil reading that poem that afternoon provided a brilliant example of what might be done, what could be reached for. His energy and invention, his narrative brilliance, were, as always, inspirational, sustaining; they encouraged me—for better or worse—to take a chance with my own efforts.

In 1997, *Michigan Quarterly Review* published an essay by Phil, "Two Journeys" which can be found in his book of essays and interviews, *So Ask*. He concludes modestly, standing shoulder to shoulder with the poets of his generation, and says, "We have told America, and the rest of the world should it care to listen, what it's been like living through this age. We have been useful."

And so my thanks, once again, to Phil for mentoring so many of us, for his encouragement and example that helped me write these poems—modest by any comparison. Nonetheless, I wanted to gather this longer work together and hopefully allow a little more light to fall on what I've seen, for whatever it might be worth.

In memory of Jon Veinberg, Phil, Jon, Ernesto, Larry, & Omar

The clouds have seen it all, in the dark
they pass over the graves of the forgotten
and they don't cry or whisper.

—*Philip Levine*

Acknowledgments

from *Blue Autumn:* Copper Beech Press

Blue Autumn—POETRY
October Visiting—*Quarterly West*
To Giordano Bruno in the Campo de' Fiori—*The Denver Quarterly*

from *Dark Matter:* Copper Beech Press

Tabula Rasa—*The Missouri Review*
Dark Time— POETRY
Dark Matter—*The Iowa Review*

from *Camino Cielo:* Orchises Press

Alisos Canyon Contract—*Crazyhorse*
The Presocratic, Surfing, Breathing Cosmology Blues . . . —*American Poetry Review*

from *Fall From Grace*: BkMk Press

4 Benches, 14 Orange Trees—*Black Warrior Review*
Death of the Poet, 1936—*Quarterly West*
Poem About the Soul: Menorca, Spain—*New Letters*
The Poverty of Clouds—*Cimarron Review*

from *Star Apocrypha:* Northwestern University Press

Zeno Said—*Passager*
Via Dolorosa—Santa Barbara, California—*SOLO*
Lost Sky—*Third Coast*

from *SKY:* Sheep Meadow Press

Mediterranean Clouds—Es Castell, Menorca—*Tiferet*
Poem Freely Accepted from the Polish—*Natural Bridge*
Five Days Rain—*The Journal*

from *And the Sea:* Sheep Meadow Press

My Parents' Photographs—*Terminus*

from *Modern History*:

Eternity—*Sentence*
Buckley y yo—*Salt Hill*

from *Rolling the Bones*: University of Tampa Press

Against Flying—*The Packinghouse Review*
M Theory and The Apothegm of Bones—*New Letters*
Thank you Note: Recent Technological & Cosmological Musings—*American Poetry Review*

from *White Shirt*: University of Tampa Press

A Little About Not Knowing Very Much—*The Southern Review*
Cantata for Clouds and Bones—*American Literary Review*
For the Saints—*Cave Wall*
Lead Penny: Early Lessons in Economics—*The Kenyon Review*

from *Varieties of Religious Experience:* Stephen F. Austin State University Press
A Sentimental Education—*ASKEW*
First Day of Retirement—Sitting in My Car at Miramar Beach During a Storm
Schrodinger's Cat—*American Literary Review*
Ontology by the Sea—*ASKEW*
Varieties of Religious Experience— *Northwest Review*
Time Travel—*New Letters*

from *Back Room at the Philosophers' Club:* Stephen F. Austin State University Press
My Problems with Math, or Why I Don't Buy Lottery Tickets—*The Packinghouse Review*
Nostalgia for the Infinite—*American Poetry Review*
Islands Moving Beneath Clouds—*New Letters*
Personal & Metaphysical Derivatives—*Solstice*
Back Room at the Philosophers' Club—*Archaeopteryx*

from *Spanish Notebook:* Shabda Press
El Cielo
Walking Around

from *The Far Republics:* Cloudbank Books
Reincarnation by the Sea—*Nimrod*
Cloud Memoir—*The Normal School*

Thanks for many years of love, support, and friendship to Nadya Brown, Gary Young, Gary Soto, and Peter Everwine.

Contents

Cloud Memoir

Blue Autumn

Santa Barbara, 1986

On a swing above the ivied sandstone wall
I swooped the level of the trees and twilight,
the gold-grey streaks and violet trumpet vines,
and with legs rowing up the evening air
my arms pushed wide and bird-pure
against the chill squeaking of the chains.
Here my first dreams and vague despair,
translating clouds to the heart's reward—
alone in my blue school sweater, my hands
were stuffed with the airy fabric of the sky,
wind-stung and light-lost toward the sea.
I was 5 years old and burning alive. . . .

Giant sycamores bent back clouds half a block
from the beach. We corner-cut the wild
ivy of a vacant lot, the watery shade of palms,
snaked our way through the lemon fields'
waist-high grass, and were here and there
beneath honeysuckle and trees of tangerines,
landing at length and round about on the sand,
traipsing our high-top sneakers unceremoniously
through tide pools and running skirts of surf.

We were boys in possession of our days,
bright and slow beneath the olive boughs.
We gazed up to where, even without a cloud,
we could see air move as surely as our blood
pumped to our fingertips as we swung
limb to limb and jumped through
the daylight for all that we were worth.

We were green then, supple as the weeds,
and chewing thick stems of sour grass mistook
the cool acids for the stuff of our young hearts.
Oh we were immune to love, wearing home
the old school jerseys after games—

over-washed and white, the numerals bleached
grey. And ganged-up and walking down
the cypressed lanes were buoyant and carefree
for we had hit and run smartly with a knee
and forearm shiver, diving through those
hoops of air—Armour, Knapp, and Stanton
Richards gunned the bootleg and halfback
reverse for our winning score across the chalk-
dust of that once and true vainglory. . . .

And though we mastered the iconography
of kickball and the Stations of the Cross,
mumbled Latin and the sorrowful mysteries
by rote, all the while our hearts churned
openly for the playing field and sun
with no second thoughts about our souls.

Now I jog around the lake and the birds
keep to themselves their secret about the sky.
I have moved through the air, mutable
as any leaf, seeing the wind's passion
for the golden nettle crowing Eugenia,
those purple berries we threw then
after school to leave our parting marks,
our lack of contrition pronounced against
the church's sun-stopped walls.

Now, I've come full circle with the citrus trees—
with the winter light rouged along these hills—
and still I am taken with that last copper streak
of cloud in a creek pool. Wandering out,
I know nothing truer than this daylight breathing
through the lemon leaves, the radiant streaming
down of it as I walk cliffs where it's all pale
dust sent up by that wind which, like me,
wants to hold everything it couldn't help
letting go. I can tell by the way it covers
each waxy perfume of laurel and pittosporum,
each evidence of salt off the spindrift breeze.
Still, I like to be here when the wind blooms

and these ungainly eucalyptus lean out
like ghosts calling in the horizon's clouds. . . .
But crows spearheaded through the coastal pines
won't let me overlook the dark, the flared
assurances of sun going dim by the evening star,
that one I bargained a faithful life away
on as a boy. Yet from that first moment
in the failing light, the complication in being
here was clear—the mountains retouched each fall
with fire, and ash sifting down as if the blind
moon had shed a rain of petals and no blessing
to sustain us finally from the dark.
Even so,
I am no one if not that boy still longing
for some gesture some life and song to ride him
out above the gloss and bay, if only for an instant
with the birds, with feathers of imagined wing
filtering dusk, that spume and flowback of days
when each passage was as evident as light,
as sure and unfinished as the sea's blue refrain.

October Visiting

for Jon Veinberg, Fresno, 1985

Even if I were certain that I was going
To heaven, I would pray God to let me go
By the longest possible route.
—Nikos Kazantzakis

Again, what great good it does
to go among these fallen leaves,
through retiring alleyways
of a sturdy merchant class,
admiring the fragrant dog roses
as they fall along a fence
and in this remind myself about beauty
despite the flush perfumes of death—
all this on the way to my friend's
porch where we'll sit among bouquets
of japonica and orange, a midday sun
through a smoke of musty sycamores.
Perhaps we'll take an early drink
for I think it was Po Chu-I, old poet
and governor, who found leisure solely
during ill health, and who wrote
how high office only profits others.
So today we'll praise the essential
precept of idleness, and for a while
do what we do best—sit here
absorbing light, watching the air move,
speculating on the apparent infinities
of space or whether there might be
violoncellos playing the foggy woods
of an afterlife. Or, more reasonably,
we might consider that wisdom
in the patience of clouds,
tireless and at peace with change
but which, when rushed, are likely to leave
all their old furniture lying in the road.
And how can we overlook the apples
weighing down the waxy boughs
while these long days unwind, for always
I find myself envying everything about
the trees—their drowsy contemplation
of the earth, and yet how all their lives

they are pulling purely away from it.

Last fall along the Arno
white spume lifted from the weir
as we climbed Brunelleschi's duomo
and then plant-like out the top
into the *Sfumato*, that tea-rose pollen
of light which floats there thick
enough to tempt you to also try
and take the air, give yourself over
to that surge and longing, to the lilac
clouds which somehow promise neither
happiness nor rain.
                                        But rain found us
in Rome with dogs lagging aimlessly
behind in the streets as we walked
all afternoon to the cemetery,
rang rust from the bell, circled
and rang again, yet no one came
to spit a curse onto the walk
for the weather or our English.
So without seeing where he's not
quite buried, or if the hand
of water has worn away his name,
we left unable to place our two sticks
of good intent together among the stones,
came away with wet leaves stuck
to our shoes, a wind knifing the blue
junipers with the unfinished
music of an ode.
                                    Then Lerici
and Cinque Terra, the steep vineyards
and airy slopes of an ethereal, white wine.
Or a Vino Santo below the lights
of Villa Marigola where they read
Byron in Italian three nights running,
where we were lulled, indolent as those
red or green skiffs nodding on the bay.
And along the breakwater that morning
we watched divers winch up a sailboat
with a broken mast—and took a last walk
to the point where we looked south
as far as Viareggio where they fished

Shelley's body out, no longer able to sing
the sea out of his veins, and sent then
its smoke up with difficulty on the dank,
impassive air.
                    And above us now
in Yosemite's cloud-high meadows,
hide-thick pods of milkweed
are breaking open of their own accord,
each with its white hosannas flying
on the short breaths of autumn—and if
there is another life and all our atoms
sail out likewise to a breeze, and if we
grow calm then, shining at some blue remove,
why should we now become preoccupied
and hurry to that insubstantial end?

Today, everything is before us, yet
invisible as the snow that will fall
in a week or two across the Sierras—
the road offers us our own grey dust
so there is no telling which way
to proceed—we could be closer to heaven,
we could be simply whistling our way out
of our skins? We have the fine nostalgia
of evening articulated in the ash trees
and for the time being we might do well
to emulate starlings in the high branches
for that last varnish of light
as they offer, without restraint,
their unmanaged choruses of faith.
For soon the days will draw short
and with them these opportunities
to eavesdrop on the convivial plants
and afterthoughts of wind; soon, we may
sit out after work with some red wine
and company against the cold and the irony
of that light submerged in our bones
will surface nonetheless and then
we will not be able to help looking up
at the rising tide of stars and feeling
the rush of all their old designs on us.

To Giordano Bruno in the Campo de' Fiori

Giordano, it's fall in Rome, overcast
for days where the sun was the only
science you were content could save us—
that primal grist we were spun about
as surely as the gold and quintessential
pears which reappear along summer boughs.
Old heretic, you were dead right
about the new astronomy, but the papists
wouldn't suffer the least celestial truth
and sent you to the flames for the fire
of your philosophies, for defying doctrine
and their dark ages, and, they thought, forever.

The century went forward on all fours
but the intricate, white architecture
of your thinking went begging until
it was bluntly cast into this statue
as overlooked here as the irregular sophists
who gather beneath it at dusk to share
some *vino da tavola* and recite
the last anthems of the flowers. . . .

Nevertheless, old firebrand, I remember
that a principle is suspired in it all,
in the dark and in our dull hearts,
in the pearl-like apotheosis of stars,
for tonight your weather-beaten outline
looms above the square as ragged
as one of the lost continents
of the moon—and across the pitched
or spired roofs, the shadow of your
infinite idea rises with the mists
like a blue wing over the bluer sky.

Tomorrow, no doubt, more of us will come
from the Midwest for favorable exchange rates,
for the ruins and the partial restorations
of romance; we'll believe without question

and so run no risk from the church.
But there's a new inquisition here,
sectarian as the old—it takes us away
from lunch under bright umbrellas
and unsettles conversation over drinks
along the Via Veneto; this red brigade
would kneecap half the globe to get
their way. So maybe it's as you say—
after all there is no real evidence
of change, and these Calvinists of anarchy
also turn a blind eye to the eternal,
and, in the fashion of the day, would not
hesitate to dump your body in the trunk.

And those who saunter by each hour,
with shopping bags and the *International*
Herald Tribune, wake one in his sleep
and he'll swear that Spinoza, your schoolboy
who stole the thunder and the themes,
pitched for St. Louis, possessed
a wicked slider and good control.
Who among us cares for the incandescence
of the spheres reified in our bones,
a plurality of worlds?
                                        And even though
Aristotle declared 9 windows to the soul,
they all reflected the extravagant clouds
or nothing more than that first cloud
Plato knew half beyond this life,
the wind-blue lake all souls float down from
with perfect knowledge of the trees—
so you divulged memory's 30 seals
and the geographies of the astral plane.
For this they gave you a robe of ash
and made you master of the clouds.

But Bruno, great speculator, where
in the long thought of God are you now?
Was there no thread of salvation
in throwing the sanctimonious dogs a bone

of contention, in having recounted
one illustrious atom of Unity?
I sit out tonight thinking it through
raising yet another Campari-soda
in your barely recovered honor, not 10 feet
from where you disappeared in smoke.
I'm waiting for the low haze to lift,
for my blood to sing a little.
Didn't you, when tied to the stake,
sense the pull of the dead planets,
the immense absence beyond your skin?
And each day now, what do you make
of this marketplace with the last
fruits of the season, the flower stalls,
olives and bread, the pungent cheeses?
All day long I make compromises
between body and soul: a bit more
asiago on the gnocchi, less red wine
after 10:00—and what I want to know,
grand necromancer, is if finally
any of it is any use?
                                        But regardless
I'm here to appreciate September nights
mystic as your gaze across the campo,
or the mute liturgies of stars appearing
at last and spinning like every petal
of fire that took you up, boundless
as belief. Can it truly be, once
and for all, all the same to you—
your bones left to the white heat
of ignorance, forsaken even as these stones
in the piazza are forsaken—this planet
coming to grief over the insubstantial
word? Do you still hold that flesh is
nothing more than the blossom of time,
of ash, and that it will fall away
before this incarnate light? That it's
all radiance *and* all dust? Or here,
on this very spot for all these days,
have we been merely treading air?

Tabula Rasa

> And endless once again it will begin:
> Life that doesn't see, speak, or think . . .
> —Nazim Hikmet

If anything it's only the wind
now that picks up our prayers
and carries them off to the sea
where it's usually March and hopes
float bluely across the surface
thorny with whitecaps there. . . .

Then, we would practice for May
Procession, and so often as we
marched up the lightless center
of the church, our small hearts
spun purely as the invisible
rose petals flower-girls were
scattering along the sandstone aisle,
purely as the sun washing through
our arms from the one window
white with daylight all that way
up the air. And for this we were excused
from class, from fractions, long division,
and the mental roadwork
of diagramming the compound-
complex sentence.
Still these nights,
the random punctuation of the stars
keeps me from seeing exactly
how, with the fragments given us,
we can, with any certainty,
trace out the lines, the blue-
prints that reveal God's agreement
in it all. At best, far against the black,
there is some chalk dust of nebulae,
a smeared handprint of light. . . .

And though we know better
than the bearskins and bones,
the fact is that the universe—lock,
stock, and expanding barrel—is red-

shifted and moving away from us,
from the fireball that sent every
primordial thing scuffling for its place
in the blank backwash of space.
Yet each time wild flowers appear
for which I have no names and
swallows weave about like algorithms
substantiating the structure of the skies,
I accept the old metaphors for life
like there's no tomorrow. Nonetheless,
there's all this dead air, untuned
radio on the frequency of the dark,
between us and our nearest neighbor
shining high in the tip of eucalyptus.
And beyond, the bright bent center
of the wheel, the anonymous read-out
that leaves stars to become
the paradigms of our desire.

These days, I just look forward
to sitting back and breathing
among wild mustard weed and radish
bloom until I'm calm and reflective
as a cloud . . . and I remember then
6th grade geography and Miss Vasquez,
the sky above La Paz in our book,
what it would be like . . . nothing
more than a chimney's ladder
of smoke anchoring that washed-out
blue, that clean slate waiting there;
the clouds, those old iconoclasts of sorrow,
sliding this way and that,
apparently above it all.
                                        But then
that first-cut fragrance of grass
takes me to the foothills east of town,
where I'm kneeling on the blacktop
for the Angelus ringing from
Our Lady of Mt. Carmel,
for the seconds it takes to recite
the formula for all we believe.

I'm driving for a hoop as soon
as I've raced through lunch;
and not long after, cruising
in a Chevy Biscayne, putting a blue moon
and constellations to the test,
desperate for any physical
evidence of love among the wild
mint leaves and manic clips of time.

But now, at the end of autumn,
late in the afternoon, burning
that intensely on any account
almost makes sense as the days
draw short and the roses dry
to the color of old light, or skin—
and the wind that freshened
in the last sprays of leaves
seems to stream more forcefully
through the trees, through the channels
in the mind, scattering the silt there
with the grey and infinitesimal float
of stellar dust.
                    And evidently
the universe *was* once rolled
into a ball—quasars imploding,
a trillion stars boxed into one star's size.
Now nothing's more abstract or absent
with itself than these black
and starless holes where everything
might one day be thrown back
into the past. Now we know
that even when galaxies collide, suns
and planets escape as gas and galactic plasma,
compress and collapse into a cloud
that can't be seen—we only blindly read it
there, pinpoint some faithless spot
where light's sucked over and erased,
much the way the voice is lost
as someone plummets down a waterfall,
though he's shouting into the white
and roaring air for everything he's worth.

Dark Time

Snow all day until
the sky is a falling
stasis—time mounting up
like the ice in windy swirls,
in spiraled, barred, or elliptical
galaxies across the window glass;
and the dim caul of air
like that star cloud
so dense it blocks
our view to the center
of the Milky Way.
                                    And so
I finally have hours to do
nothing but settle back
and remember what it was
exactly I used to be
so obsessed about—what went
climbing out of my heart
pure as the purple flames
of bougainvillea up the sun-
bleached stucco of my youth?

But my mind draws blanks,
like one of those radio dishes
in the deserts of New Mexico
that's trained on the deep
and abstract heart of space
on a day when only static
interference is skimmed off stars.

I should be tracing out
thoughts like the scientist
at the telescope during "dark time"—
those nights when the moon is down
and the least heavenly body
ignites on the photo plates—
the lost spark and slow burn,
flotsam of matter's first wreck still
blasting by the floorboards of time.

He plays dot-to-dot, looking for
a little linkage, some new move-
ment across the firmament's
held breath by which he might
name the unknown, say
it's a shiny grain smaller,
somewhat like the light beams
we're divided down to quarks
and neutrinos, all these small
threads coming loose off
the long sleeves of the dark.
But I sit here passive
as any receiver, silent
as the cogwheels of the void
grinding blindly away, barely
vital as that dust and star floss
lifted just enough into our air
so we might appreciate the light.

I think I like it better
the way Aristotle had it—
all the planets pushed around
the perfect earth by angels
on concentric crystal spheres,
everything self-referential,
parochial as the blue.
Even the Egyptians and Chinese
saw stars as little lamps
set out at the same distance
from the earth, though each
deciphered different animals crawling
in the light's bare bones.

Memories are often like this
group of asteroids discovered
bumping about the belt
between Jupiter and Mars;
darker than anthracite, no brightness
going out from them as they bob
and weave among ice and refraction,
tear away and are known only
by a bulge in the force fields

around planets of moons.
And staring now out this grey
glass, I catch on my reflection,
and recall that time when I was 12,
the cabinet mirrors on each side
of the bathroom sink tilting
out enough so I could see
my face duplicate and recede,
framed smaller back to a pinpoint
in space until I closed my eyes
only to hear in that darkness
the unconscious march of Latin
drilled into my brain, the ancient
certainty of the dead proclaiming
new and conquered boundaries.
But, when I opened my eyes,
I saw the same rainclouds
that kept me in all day, holding
there like dull frescoes on a wall,
like thumbprints in ash—only
a remote glimmer of intention
behind the confines of the sky.

Dark Matter

> Beneath the music from a farther room.
> —Eliot

Drawn out past
our local orbits,
past street lamps pushing
the night back beyond
a walkway's sleeping roses
and the cul-de-sac,
we are once more
none the wiser
unearthed in the fact
that 90% of the universe
is not radiating? All the non-
luminous chaff tossed off
the kernels of light—all that
is really most all of it
as thinks now add up
and will not appear.

I've arrived at middle age
in a moonless month,
and though the heavens are clearer
for that, I'm still seining
among the stars without a clue.
But somewhere, it's out there,
chockablock about the blue
and unfathomable fire
of quasars, dodging
crab nebulae, white dwarfs—
so many black asterisks bobbing
in the dimples of gravity,
the relative bend and sink holes
of space.
As far as I can see
it's as if the cosmos were
10% music, a leitmotif
or gloss harmony
spun out against the dread-
naught of silence. Life slipped
in somewhere, sparkling,

say, on the 10th-notes—
one metronomic pause
between the redshift of galaxies,
a few white notes, reversed
out on the black cosmic sheet,
composing the only music
we have ever made sense of.
Mozart, you heard it said,
took dictation from the stars,
progressions of chords, arias and
divertimento arriving transfixed
in his mind as the constellations
first inscribed by the Chaldeans.

After dinner, the pinwheel
of the Milky Way uncoils
its spangled shirttails across
the back lots of a universe
10 billion light-years end to
end—and now when looking out,
I picture that distance
like a luminous clothesline
upon which all blind space is hung,
though we've long been told
that it's all brilliance, all
radiance and a shower of light
at the end. . . .
                        For now,
our thoughts could be nothing
more than asteroids, circling
the fission of the mind—sand,
boulders, small worlds; the lost,
the faint, the fresh as blood—
silica, carbonaceous compounds,
nickel and iron—everything
we might be or all we'll never
become. Yet whatever it is
we've done shines often, persists,
and comes back to us like comets
slowly wearing down on their

icy and elliptical tracks.
It all hangs with us, a worry
in the air—spalls of cold light
scudding among the turgid
gravel of the dark.
                                        Perhaps
like bits of smoky celluloid
negatives with their pale-
as-paper figures, we wait to be
held up once more against
a brightness to begin again?

Or perhaps it's that we drift
airily around star to star,
their billion silver keys
every brilliance there is to tell—
that jangling all the obsequies
we will ever hear?
                                        Maybe
this is why I go for walks
more often now at night,
whistling some tune
I dimly recall,
if only for distraction's sake,
for the circumstantial evidence
of my breath with its faint
refraction of star dross
bright in a cloud before me. . . .

Alisos Canyon Contract

A child in the affluence
of space and leaves,
I walked out agreeing
with the trees. At my command
the grand inheritance of the sky,
an affidavit summoned
above the sandstone and
perpetual oaks, a blank page
in back of the coastal range
on which clouds scribbled
my three initials—
proof of everything
left to me under the sun.

I hiked or rode a bike there
for the day-long business
of climbing house-size rocks,
monitoring the white
surf-curls and backwash
of indigent clouds.
                                        Cars slid by
down the distant road, so many
fish shining through their deep
and watery gates. My ambition
was to gather waist-high foxtails
with my open hand. My distractions
were tangerines burning
like day-time stars in the tops
of the one foothill grove,
a buzzard tilting in his dark patrol.
No one knew me
as I knew myself
in my green and adaptable heart.
Cochise, Robin Hood, Johnny Ringo,
The Cisco Kid. I lived
those lives at once,
and no one quicker
to draw against shadows
or track the venomless lizards
to their hideouts in stone,
to send a silver-tipped arrow

into the soft belly of a log.
Who knew better the cutoffs
and switchback paths, the crossing
rocks in pools, the free-fall stanzas
of the creek high into the hills
and all the lost Himalayas?
I believed as I was told—
anyone who wished could
have it all. The evidence
was plain as daylight
as far as I could see—
there was plenty, and plenty to share,
would always be—this was easy
as the air.
And as if that too
were a place you could go,
just by saying so, I stood still
in the wind and claimed
the franchise of the light
across the breathing fields.

Where did I go once
sycamores set their last star-
yellow leaves against autumn
and gave way to the grey
murmur of the boughs?
Sunset, and the yucca
and agapanthus blooms
are at a loss to say.
Here, a dull dusk covers
the day's remains, copperish
as the edge of a coin. Riffraff
of the lesser skies, sparrows
and mockers, offer up a run-down
of my immediate life and times,
the scratch in the dust
I've made, the here and now
beyond the softened margins,
the sea-colored needles
of tamarisk and pine—
the incessant breeze that just picks
at the surface of things.

And if I look, as it has become
my weakness to look, for something
to correspond, to pull into myself—
lure and sparkling spinner—
it's one star shooting lengthwise,
a nylon line cast past the surf,
a flare across the smudge pot night
that goes under with the dead
weight of hope. . . . And memory
sputtering against a screen,
the early outline of that dark
for an instant or so silvered
into smoke—spokes to a wheel
of vaporous gauze.
                                        Sky with all
the house lights left on,
floating basin of the Milky Way
shifting left, footloose
in its freight and no place
now for pity, reflexive as palm leaves
sprung into the windy night.
                                                    This
is the little prayer that wakes me,
calls me back from a landscape
where trees are not cold
enough to be quiet,
has me up early with the wind,
repeating everything. . . .

I want to tell myself
this is all there has to be—
sky with its citrus glaze,
salt off the spindrift stars,
an aquifer of light beyond
the old street to the sea—
and a gale off the bay,
the belled catalpa leaves
asking, Do you still want to fly?
And the green knowledge
of those sail-shaped leaves
inscribed on the evening's
parchment sheen, where
finally the blue life of air
is forfeit again into my arms.

The Presocratic, Surfing, Breathing Cosmology Blues . . .

When the great waters went everywhere, holding the germ, and generating lights, Then there arose from them the breath of the gods.

— "Hymn to the Unknown God" from the *RIG VEDA*

Let's get real gone. —Elvis Presley

The idea of an infinite number of stars brought Newton to his knees, for that would turn
the sky into a blazing haze—flame rises naturally—and so reasoned Empedocles,
Homer, and Anaxagoras who filled the farthest reaches with fiery light. . . .

The back pages of cosmic history blow open, a bright litter of particles swimming in
the blue backwash of quasars, kernels back at the beginning smoldering finally
through to us now, telescopes probing not just into space
but into time. . . .

So galaxies in the Coma Cluster appear to us as they looked seven hundred million years
ago, about the time the first jellyfish—its own roseate nucleus of cells and
spinning arms—was developing on earth,

where, some years later, I would turn up at 9, walking tip toe along Miramar Beach,
avoiding the pink and scattered nebulae washed up for a mile around—
a sting like hot coals, a cold quivering mass of burning stars.

Or where I sit now, admiring a sugar maple, flag of impending flame, angelic breathing
we attribute to trees as we bivouac at the perimeter of nothing as instrumental
as beauty, and are mainly recursive, among other elemental things.

What wouldn't it be worth to have time again to worry about incursions of fog over
the blacktop, the starry orange groves dissolving on the slow drive to school,
to worry about the spelling of grey or gray, or Mississippi, the mysterious
lives of Saints, a laundry line of levitating miracles commemorated
along the church's tomb-dark walls

where beeswax candles, placed cross-wise on my throat, would save me from choking
on the bones of fish, and holy water sprinkled along the air keep a sea-wide
iniquity from seeping under the closed door of the soul so I might be
admitted to the beatific company of clouds, the clear apertures
in an updraft of wind.

And I in fact sometimes pondered the unsubstantiated Soul—invisible, but something
just the same—like a glass of water filled to different levels during music class,
sounding a high or low note as a finger orbited the transparent rim.

Or in back bookcases, The World Book Encyclopedia, all the blank space edging dark
columns of letters proclaiming the Hittites' fierce knowledge of iron, the Code
of Hammurabi, The Lighthouse at Pharos, and the first space capsule
burning like a thimble of coal in the stratosphere.

Yet, when we think about it, our youth lasts all our lives, trailing us like a comet tail of ice
and dust, or the way angels, like knots in a rope of light, are still let down to us
from the dark in Caravaggio's first "St. Matthew," the one sent up
in flames in the bombing of Berlin

whose atoms are still associated in the grey haze that constantly resettles that sky, re-
claiming its dust in the thin half-light of loss, in the past riding that freight
of light out to a universe where all things are contingent upon each other,
upon, as Anaximander had it, "The Indefinite."

There's much that matters in that dark where my hands are full of the brilliant dross
off the recent edge of discovery, data no one in school had the least idea existed
when I took my D in General Science.

Now I'm writing it all down—Vacuum Genesis, Lookback Time—thinking I'm getting
somewhere, only to realize I need another course in Italian Cinema just to
make the metaphors make sense!

Was it Luchino Visconti's *Death in Venice* or Vitorio De Sica's *Brief Vacation?* Dirk
Bogarde on the Lido coughing out the dark matter of his lungs for some blond
boy in a bathing suit as Mahler's symphony moved like a cloud
of melting glass over the sea,

or that beaten angel of a housewife escaping her truck driving, mule-headed husband
in Torino with black stars on her X-rays, a silt of light slowing in her veins
which took her up to the state sanitarium in the snowy Alps, a comet-quick
brush with a younger man reconstituting the rose-colored clouds
of her lungs, but sending her finally back?

And I remember holding my breath, the universe expanding inside my lungs as I was
tumbled like a rag in the spin-cycle of ten foot surf a quarter mile off shore,
riding the point break at Rincon and plunged into the white salt-roar
of froth, my chest burning as I shot up to that heaven

of air above the surface—and while heaven could, in theory, have been anywhere,
it was there that minute as I swallowed the air's cool light, mindless of every
molecule and the constant state of flux all things are in.

And regardless of the frenzy of atoms and the sub-atomic voids, I'd have sold my soul
for my dinged-up plank, anything to hold to and fill my flattened pipes
before the next wave with its five feet of churning soup rolled in,
beneath which I'd have to dive, count ten, and come up again
gasping toward a low tide of rocks.

In college, staring out past the spires of Italian cypress, wind bending the invisible
blue beyond the second story classroom windows, the thick glass sinking,
soaked with old light, the Presocratics were proclaiming the single source
to everything. Half conscious, at swim in the 60s, I was reaching
for the first idea that would keep my head above dark waters.

And, like Einstein, whom I hadn't read, I didn't bother about the details and showing
my work—all the math and elegant equations—I just wanted to know what was
on God's mind when he shook up this *boule de niege* and let time-space
float out and gather here with our little neighborhood of
respiration and recourse to nothing but light?

But at 19 I had recourse to little beyond beer and the bylaws of poker. Was it or wasn't it
air? Aneximines proclaimed everything was—just reified and condensed—while
Thales assured us all things were water, and I'd seen plenty of that.

They both fared better than Heraclitus who favored fire—for, the obvious consideration
of our weight aside, as air, we were almost spirits already, and shouldn't we
shine then at last among the aethers? Yet sinking in the specific gravity
of over 40 years, the best I come up with most nights is moonlight
through the trees, its mist lifting almost imperceptibly
through the leaves. . . .

It turns out the Ionians were not that far off track: cosmic radiation—the original red
hot atomic spin and background hum—can be tuned-in from any cold rocks
in a universe 95% back-filled with a dark and missing theoretical matter—
that bang and microwave broadcast even the deaf sill hear. . . .

And so, I have little more on hand than air and a forecast of air where it is unlikely
I'll find myself free of the old aptitude of starlight to break our hearts—though
I look into the infinite, the nothingness, the nowhere, and the dark
as if I recognized the light in its last disguise.

4 Benches, 14 Orange Trees

Mahon, Menorca

I'm watching the old men on these 4 back–to-back
slat benches, beneath 7 pairs of Valencia orange trees
spaced so a green air infuses the 2 pedestrian streets
that join here for the square in Mahon. It is instructive, and,
to some degree reassuring—they've known each other since
they could first call out down these stone streets,
though in truth they look as if they've always been old,
as if they remember the Carthaginians and the Moors.
And listening to them I hear what could be a bit of both
spun on the choppy syntax and swallowed vowels—
undercurrent of Old French, Catalan cutting Spanish down to size.
Their rhythms and repetitions make a music out of morning—
4 or 5 crowding a bench, on the edge, facing 1 who stands
to lecture commanding a rhetoric that appeals to clouds
and is supported by the fierce birds of his hands. . . .

They have given up cigars, have listened darkly and at length
to doctors, something the younger men dismiss lighting up
in banks, restaurants, buses, jewelry stores—at all times
and everywhere asserting themselves in smoke and neglect
as if life and death did not apply. Not these old ones.
They cherish this little place to congratulate each other
on the weather, the lack of wind, on continuing to breathe,
comfortable in the citrus-scented hours. They did their work,
that's done—hands thick as slabs of bacon tell you that.

And work, I think, is not the subject, they have moved to art—
the democratic crafts of greeting, praising the day in 5 salutations.
They love to stop someone and grasp both hands, pat the shoulder
until the litany is complete. The same when one of them leaves
for his afternoon's soup and squid—waves and salutes across the square,
"deos" for "adios" or half a dozen other ways to sing goodbye.
They've paid the price of the fields or the sea in full
so that they may enjoy their idea of gentlemanly apparel:
cardigans in green or brown, rayon dress shirts, ties in muted stripes,
pressed flannel slacks with cuffs. You'd swear each was doing well
in business for himself somewhere in Ohio in 1958. And so
if an orange falls, they ignore it and go on gesturing to heaven
or the empty sky, or empty heaven—go on filling the square

with their half songs and agreements, proclaiming the dozen
truths anyone should know; having arrived at this station
in life—indicated by such sartorial splendor—a collective pride
does not allow stooping to windfall fruit.
All morning
they are here, doing nothing for as long as the air holds out,
happy despite a good part of everything behind them, gone down
that country road where dust catches in daylight and smudges
out the blue a bit, where once the heavy wagons cut ruts across
this flat table of stone. And they know that the road's end
is out there—they hear the rag man with his cart coming
and quickly close their shutters on the street and his calls,
returning to the dim kitchen for another coffee, to the small
courtyard where one canary is still singing for the sun.

At the end of these trees, a street lamp holds a white halo
against the sky, but I'm not sitting beneath it working out
the square root of wisdom nor have I arrived here in my youth
ready to rebuild a land of crumbling walls. No, I go unnoticed
in my jeans, and sport coat from the charity shop across the way.
I could be any one not at work this day, or taking the 11:00 break
for café and *ensaimades,* so casual is a business day anyway
which pauses over 3 hours each afternoon.
I'm taking account
of half of my life is all, grateful for the time out, this sky's clean slate
in front of me, the disinclination here to figure out final sums.
I'm thinking of friends far to the west who still meet 40 years later
at the breakwater to fish where a line has no chance of reaching
past the waves—talking, as they used to say, just to hear themselves talk.
Mechanics, lawyers, bread truck drivers—what can it matter now?
20 years in academia, no job important enough to ruin your heart for
by middle age. To be almost happy now, I need only look 3 feet above
my head to the fruit hanging half gold half green or a little higher
to the constant sun and keep breathing as evenly. I want to see Murillo's
"St. Francis in the Kitchen of the Angels" and know again what it takes
to feed a soul on only mist and stone. I am trying to take a little lesson
from these leaves blown both ways and coming back calmly to themselves.

But damn, Burt Lancaster has died! I leave the country once
every 10 years and this is the kind of thing that happens. ZAM,

just like that. I only saw the headline in a Spanish movie tabloid:
BURT LANCASTER MUERTO. Not a clue. He must have had some
good years left? But who ever knows all the factors working
against you—silent as air in an island cove no one is breathing?
Look away for a minute and things go sailing over the edge.

How does it all add up? For example, the coats in the charity shop
in Mahon are the same ones found in Fresno or Philadelphia—
world-wide someone's got his hand in it all, keeps an eye out,
has distribution, contacts and associates, knows who does tweed
in Ireland, serge in Toledo, decides about the brown polyester pinstripe,
the grey worsted with large red checks, the houndstooth, the gabardine,
and how everyone without real money will have to sport these
mild atrocities new and second-hand for close to 50 years.

So who was taking care of business then when Burt went out?
He never flinched. And lightning, fire, thunder, who ever grinned
that many teeth as completely in malice, knowledge, or reckless joy?
And hell, Burt had religion to boot. To believe in the longevity of desire,
you only had to hear him—in his 60s then—in *Atlantic City* as he recited
the ritual of Susan Sarandon's bathing, the rinsing of arms, breasts,
and neck with soap flakes and lemon after her shift at the seafood bar.
There are people who'd bury bodies under football stadiums for that
kind of eloquence and fervor. In *1900* he didn't hesitate to put
his 2 bare feet squarely into cow shit to make the scene between
the patron and the peasant girl work. With reason and patience
he taught a kid to cook garlic shrimp, a sparrow to have the fortitude
of a prize fighter. On the beach in black & white he loved Deborah Kerr
as no one ever would again. I even bought him in the bad westerns
and war films which were all, in the 50s, Hollywood decided we would watch.

Who can we look to now to stick his chin squarely out at fate
and duck its long left hook? Jack Lemon, Kirk Douglas, Tom Cruise?
True enough, there's still Tony Quinn who has the charisma
in one hand to give a story life or a life a story by just raising that hand
carefully to the sky, knowing what a dicey thing a soul can be.
He has the power but not the glory according to the number crunchers,
not the rating anymore to land a leading role. Word is, he's trying
to get a film off the ground on his own—Tolstoy at the end where
he finds religion, or rather *is* religion—starting his own church,
going about the countryside on a train, his car turned into a chapel,
coming to the window in the white tunic weighed down with gold thread,

mystical until death as the snowfall light spinning over the black firs.
Burt began in film noir, in *The Killers*—by the end he knew what was
coming for him, but was clear, sure, calm, and always came back.

There is still life ahead—ample perhaps, gregarious or serene
at a simple level, as these men in Mahon—all who have outlived
Burt Lancaster—demonstrate who do not need these lovely oranges
from the trees of Valencia. If I put the pressure and ambition
behind me, I could well make do with an orange for each pocket
of my coat, a free, small space to breathe, figuring I have
maybe 40 years left if I retreat to the provinces, drink and eat
with moderation the fruits of the earth, thereby remaining
on the earth.
Counting, that's what I've been doing. Obsessive,
spinning like this globe, heart in a cage. Type-A, trying to read
every schedule of the air, get there first or finally. A pocket full
of paper confetti, that's all—throw it into the wind. And what was it
that took Burt? Too much work, high/hard living, stroke or heart?
Sure, all of the above. Star exploding, nova in the small galaxy
of the cells, which, for all practical purposes is where all
those stars are anyway. Flash. Then, against the dark, that nothing
that every bit of worry finally amounts to, plays back—reel to
reel—a life as you know it in time before the blind and
seemingly unmarked distance dissolving beyond the trees.

Death of the Poet, 1936

> *I don't want to hear again that the dead do not lose their blood . . .* —Federico Garcia Lorca

Despite the black fuse ticking in the blood,
the days like fine ash sifting sunward
through our atoms and the weak theory of flesh,
despite the clear cloud of the soul hovering
like a late afternoon moon over the hills of the past,
and a wind dictating its deep songs through
the sorrowful postures of the elms,
who ever stands up, detached as starlight,
as the great lies of great fiction,
and with philosophy calmly drinks the cold cup
of his own death—the immediate future,
a fusillade of bullets, comes biting out black
space and time, the only signal to the landscape
a fogged breath, staggered and homeless as a cloud?

Who doesn't come to morning with some hope
shining on his shirt sleeves, not of course like a star,
but at least like an old scar burning on the body
of the will, like a little gleam from an old coin
rubbed across a white cuff, and there,
in that moment, doesn't embrace some shred of belief
in the timelessness of his bones, in the essential power
of his two shaking hands to cup water and life
the first gift of the earth to his face and see
that face still shining there against the sky—
or the power of his voice, its influences
of rivers and green seas, to still call the hours
to order like the strings of the guitar and be
acknowledged along the avenues and in cafés?
Who could imagine the hives of the mind, its blue
electricity spinning to a stop even as the eyes
proclaim the fire-fed tributaries of dawn?
                                                            No one.
Not one of us in the ordinary assignments of our lives,
for, doing what little we can, what does it matter
when the knock at the door comes for the wrong reason,
for the dark heart of reason, or no reason, really, at all?
Dioscorso Galindo Gonzalez, schoolmaster and republican,

beloved by his students, but denounced as a "dangerous enemy"
by a secretary to the local municipal corporation.
Joaquin Arcollas Cabezas and Francisco Galadi Melgar,
minor bullfighters and anarchists, "undesireables"
delivered to the Black Squad—those boys from the Catholic
middle class, sons of merchants, lawyers, bankers
who had *carte blanche* to butcher "reds."
These citizens were driven out the road to Alfacar in darkness
while Manuel de Falla wept in his moonless courtyard
and listened to the stars fall without music,
the firing from the cemetery in Granada going on
in small bursts through the early hours of morning.
Near the spring Fuente Grande the assassins shot
their victims and rolled the bodies in to the olive groves
on the right hand side of the road as you come from Viznar:
two bullfighters, a schoolmaster with a wooden leg,
one in a white shirt with a loose artistic tie.

There is no reason to forget. Not 60 years.
Not the Alhambra with its amusing gardens
and mosaics. Not the coach tours to the gypsy caves
nor the one fine restaurant beneath the aqueduct.
Not socialism or the EEC. His father did not forget.
He took the extortion note they forced him to write—
a request for a donation of 1,000 pesetas to the army—
into exile in New York, where for the last nine years
of his life, he carried it in his wallet—the final thing
the poet ever wrote.
Let us say more than Fate,
Falangists, or even Franco and fascism. Let us say
Ramon Ruis Alanzo, junior office who acted
"on his own initiative" arresting the poet for,
among other things, broadcasting to the Russians
on a secret radio. Let us say Juan Luis Trescastro,
accomplice of Ruis Alanzo, who boasted the next morning
of helping at the execution, of firing "Two bullets
in his arse for being a queer." Also Gov. Valdez
who claimed the poet was already taken off
when the documents for his release were produced
and he was still in custody upstairs. And Gen Quipe de Llano,
commander of the Nationalists in Andalusia, who, over the phone,
gave his dark code: "Give him coffee, plenty of coffee."

And let us not forget the bourgeoisie of Granada
who ground that coffee, who face to face, executed
well over 2,000 of their countrymen and women
to eliminate left wing opposition—doctors, professors,
town councilors, schoolmasters, workers and trade unionists.
And who did so with gusto, terror, and the great moral certainty
of the right, who rang bells, kept their saints' days, gave to the church,
and lived out their lives comfortably denying everything.
In the blue clay of the barranca of Viznar, five bad miles of road
to the north, the dead were shoveled into shallow graves.
Later pines were planed to cover the mounds and hollows,
to erase the few stones placed there. Later still,
Franco ordered the trees cut and the ground leveled
to make that place invisible to those who kept coming.
But he could not dismiss the sparrows who hung on like remorse,
unseen in the olives and roadside pines, confabulating like ghosts
in low clouds. He could not stop the fine grit of salt
falling in the steady accusation of wind.

He sleeps his sleep of apples, each with its small lock
of light, the sleep of the ocean, moonlight dissolving
into it. He sleeps with that gold on his lips and hears
nothing of the torments of the reeds or the dead child,
his mouth of water beneath a white camellia
that has become the moon. He dreams the dream
of the mountain beyond the valley of rain,
and does not hear the long silence continue to issue
from the windows of the state. He does not see the blind
white eyes of dawn as each day the birds bear witness
from the bloody stars of their throats.

Poem About the Soul: Menorca, Spain

The single engine plane lifts up from San Luis
above the sun-blocked windsock there and circles
Es Castell. Each day this winter he laps the local air,
six or seven wide slow loops, hanging on the under-
carriage of a cloud as we look up after it, and the trailing
contralto threading the singed evening sky. Higher,
a jet's red contrails scar the irradiant blue which is still
the sole province of Esteban Murillo, his true unworldly
subject which lifted him a level in the world higher
than the lives of saints. Higher still, the invisible
galaxies blaze blindly away, redshifted toward the empty
space of space. . . .
                                        Cloud remnants scatter clock-like
about the sun, and the plane, like a rusty second hand,
passes over the humming line of roofs, the fused black
branches of the palms.
                                        Out here, I feel there's something
I've forgotten—name, address, directions on the dresser
left among wadded bills and change, in a city so far back
I can barely see the brown exhausted afternoon drift
over the wide sidewalks and turtle-back sedans, someone
in shirt sleeves and tie leaning from a window above
the Rexall Drug, reading want ads for a city to the west.
Yellow stoplight sagging on a wire at the corner
of a five-floor walk up—there's a full tank of gas
in the Oldsmobile, and he goes. . . .
                                                            I walked out here
pockets empty except for a lucky piece from Canada
saved at the cold end of my 45th year—a Loon, a half bright
hard metal dollar intended to approximate gold. It's as close
to gold as it is to luck. All the same I walk along and whistle
tunes the air waves would have carried to the old radio
on that dresser—"My Blue Heaven" or "I've Got the World
On a String." Late 40s blithe romance and 50s upbeat impossibility,
a mix so I keep the ironies in play, so I can remember my father
in his brown slacks and tasseled suede shoes, so I remember
not to expect things like a kid in Woolworth's in 1952.
All of this reminding me that I am not even 45 anymore
and am wearing some other man's coat, a once snazzy houndstooth

tweed I snagged in the charity shop. It goes with jeans, and
was only $4.00, which saves those wadded bills for a *menu del dia,*
one of the amazing three-course lunches which, for 6 bucks,
keep the body and soul together all day—so I'm lucky after all.

It can't just be the sun I'm after here, not in winter, not all
this way? Rather, the long term effect is what I want
to know about—how terminal is it? Leaning on my rented balcony,
I pronounce the precepts of two languages against the wind,
and what does it get me? Not one inch closer to the clouds
than rent money already has—not grace or insight nor reprieve
from the self-important past. Only the slim notion of a feeling
now that might sustain me despite the Tramontana wind
descending from the north with its jack hammer breath.
And I can take that, the scouring of the backdrop here
in the middle of the sea. Anywhere else, we're ruining
the sky like there's no tomorrow—Los Angeles, the Amazon,
the faces of men and beasts eaten away by the sour air
in Athens, the arms of caryatids so frail they can't hold
their own hands up let along the porticos of cataleptic gods.

We're at the mercy of the light, the plants breathing out
our breath—stop that and no one questions the first invisible
thing. We're not going into the sky, no going anywhere
but back to the enduring dull compounds of dust. This pearl-rich
winter sky might be something though, some sample of the form
it took to fix one life firmly within another? This sky
over the Mediterranean blown clear, beeswax bright—
I let it coat my palms, holding them up for the final gloss
skinning the blue edge of the pines.
And I have to ask myself,
as the famous wind prevails, as bleached laundry across
the rooftops flails arms and legs, as the waves whip up
and overrun a white fishing skiff until it barely glimmers
back its opaque shape from the glass-blue bottom of the cove,
what has already taken the past and added it to the dark
without looking back to see if someone might be standing
on a cliff trying to strike a match, or turning on his lamp
by the chair to red Lao-tzu or Charles Péguy's riddles
in support of God, or even pouring out a small glass of *fino*
to measure the bronze horizon line?

In the esplanada,
in the streets, a hundred kids are waiting for sundown—
two to a motorbike, smoking in groups on the street corners
like something from the 50s. Like them, why should I care
if the plane keeps going around the small sky of San Luis
like a lost planet? Only this: that it comes down with grace
and with the dark so that they may go about unknown
into the unknown with the one blessing of the night.
But I am consoled so long as I hear that high murmur
plying the apparent nothing above us, burning in the cold
climate there that it climbs continually to know.

And the line of old men without a boat, or a job on one
anymore, who sit on the stone bench cut into the cliff
of Cala Corb, they also pay the plane no mind and do not
look to the sky with questions. They keep their regular
positions each day until the sun goes. It is easy to look
at them and make a case for the sleeping collective soul
as they speak to each other or to the sea, gesturing
as if they were still untangling the nets or testing wind.
Other than the sea, most have never been off the island.
Not going. All the death and life and rain falling from this
only sky, fall, as they see it, in the acknowledged
democracy of wind. For all intents and purposes, they know
what's coming, are content to offer themselves to this light,
hoard it within as they walk home, holding it in
their empty hands. Enough of this, enough days among
enough friends and perhaps you grow calm, never lose it—
the luster never goes altogether from you?
Near the window
I slice some lemon into a glass and cover the luminous
rind with an ounce of dark *Cynar,* that dense liquor
distilled from the artichoke, a drink that holds
the same burnt color as that relic of the saint's tongue
on a spike. I think too of the thistle and its black seeds,
the half-bitter essence igniting in me like a slow fuse.
I think of the small plane easing down to land, the old
engine shaped like a thistle flower, a crown of grease
and oil sparking, keeping it burning, bright enough to fly.

I remember Fellini saying, "Sometimes pulling a little tail,
one finds an elephant at the other end." And so while life
turns out glorious in bits, impossible in stages, imponderable
finally at the one level above sorrow which we all want
to know, we breathe and hope we are not deceived by the music
of the trees, the reeds strung with rain, the unscripted stars
we cannot escape. For one thing, the pointed hats, the wings
and silver replications of the moon are all taken in at the end.
For another, that road along the sea where the processions and
makeshift band turned back is the same one you set out on,
thinking of the ten thousand things you would have out there
among the lights.
Federico was laid in state high in front of
the azure sky from his last film: angels in coveralls and painters' caps
going about up there, touching up the background, a full orchestral
arrangement of clouds indicating perhaps a city of white aspirations
above all the visible poverty of the grass and unpaved lanes.
And here, by the shore, the sea churns away and articulates
a silence never found when gone into the wilderness or
onto the high roofs at dawn. You look west into the white fire
of the sky, and a small plane disappears, a pinpoint in the sun.

The Poverty of Clouds

Anything is enough if you know how poor you are.
—Larry Levis

We want things. Right now.
Because whatever we have
on earth—this railing for example
around a small balcony four flights up—
never holds back the sky's impoverished weight,
or the predictable transaction of morning
offering neither mystery or revelation.

But I'm at that age where I'll just settle
for my breath, the clear enclave
of memory at this blue hour
where there are only two restaurant workers
waiting at the bus stop, in the cold,
their white kitchen smocks flapping
in the wind. And they look, really,
nothing at all like angels,
each holding his old Adidas sneakers—
work shoes bruised with grease—
speaking a Spanish
I always half understand.

The railing bleeds rust through
the tacky surface of the paint,
and my thumb prints add up
like the first dull clouds floating by
against the flat backdrop of air—
the only reliable company
desire ever keeps. . . .

I'm gone now long enough from home
that no matter how much I want
to walk down State Street to Canon Perdido,
turn right for the California Theater,
go up to the kid left waiting for his ride
and pat him on the shoulder,
I should know that he hasn't stood there
for 30 years, that soon it will be dark
and the same low sky over the mesa

will send up a smattering of clouds
like feathers from a pigeon
just struck by a car.
And it shouldn't matter anymore
what happened to my one pair
of Florsheim wing tips, the ones I saved
all summer for so I'd have what passed
for style that last year in school
when we were all wearing white socks,
those polished cordovans gleaming ridiculously
beyond my means. I must have worn them
to death, or to dust, or left them behind
when I went off to college, and one day
some poor soul at the Salvation Army
spotted them and shined the toes
with the greasy sleeve of his raincoat
before he shuffled off deliriously
despite the uneven heels,
the ground down soles.

When didn't we want something
from the world every day
regardless of the fact that some sky
off in the future was filling
with loss, waiting to resemble itself
as vaguely as a cloud?
This would be fate, out of the past,
a little fog burning off the coast,
a lesion on your calf, invisible,
growing there since you were 7—
the damage, the Dr. says, all done
before you're 20—time just keeping
everything from happening at once.

But there was something
glowing in me back there—
not 100 watts of wisdom, for I sat
in the back of class, day-dreaming
out the window, watching for the clouds
that would spell rain and let us out early.

Nor was it a brief glimmer
of grace falling on my hands
through the high windows of the church
that lit the quick fuses in my veins
and shot me out of there for what
blood alone was worth.
Wisdom would not have helped
my dog-eager heart which loved
the slow down-sifting of days
and what few illuminated moments
the angels in their grey uniforms doled out—
the extra recess after mass, glazed
donuts and hot chocolate, the sugar rush
that had us leaping from trees and off
lunch tables yelling, Jesus, Holy Smokes!
I went around looking up and expecting
the next wonderful thing to appear.
So if anyone remembers air—the invisible
celebrity of breath—it's me; it was pure
as high as the clouds then went—
my arms full of the mystic
sources of dust and a bit of wind going red
over the dark shoulders of the oaks.

Above the peaks of the Santa Ynez
the late clouds were ivory and belled as yucca blooms—
that calligraphy, oh, I could read it clearly then,
could diagram every inference
in my grey uniform shirt as I raced out of class
with a hand-colored map of yellow, green, and blue
on which I'd inscribed Addis Ababa, Constantinople,
and Timbuktu. I climbed the acacia saying
those names among the confabulating birds,
commanding for a moment all that space
and time waving from my hand,
aided and abetted by the sky.
Where else was I going?
Everything rushing by,
leaving only a small hesitancy
on the air, the way the Southern Pacific "Daylight"
swooshed past at 4:15 each day
and was gone straight south

toward the copper sun which gleamed
like the penny I'd placed on the tracks
and never found. . . . I stood there
until I could see nothing but a vacant haze,
until the rails—so polished by the grinding insistence
of steel—mirrored the sky and quit singing.

Back at that sky, clear and colorless,
the first of autumn, wild ivy lined white
at the edges—let's just sit there and see
if the camphor leaves will speak,
will intercede with the rain clouds,
with their old cavalcade of admonitions,
if we will ever escape that longing
for happiness, that landscape of old light
everlasting in our blood. . . .

By the bear-shaped lake of Oso Flaco
stars rose yellow as the coreopsis,
I collected whale bone, seal spine and sand dollars
that turned quickly back to sand.
In Ensenada, children reach out, begging
as if their arms were broken,
their cotton shirts dirty as the dim sky
as they arrive on every corner,
                                        their skin
dark as the air beneath every shade tree
in Roeding Park, where no one now,
I think, sits on that picnic table
beneath the starving redwood,
opening a box of Marlboros, lighting one
after another with controlled resignation,
exhaling perfectly detached rings
that dissolve into nothing,
into blue halos that hold a second
as if there were something celestial
in the first punished light of dawn,
a cloud of smoke, or ordinary despair.

I only have to return here once

in a great while to update my notes
on the composition of grief,
the insolvency of even the most
casual desire—the usual green paint
built up over who once loved whom
carved into the wood, initials,
dates, a star drifting off the edge . . .
and overhead, stars falling like small change
through the hands of the dark.

I routinely underestimate
the physics, the failure of particles
which account for us, for loss,
but not in any measurable sense
for that handful of Ones
left on the counter where he's
drinking alone, and peacefully,
and not for that plank of the park table
where no one sits flicking a cigarette
with its comet trail of sparks
toward the trash can or Blackstone Ave.
where he'll at last head out for home,
all the windows of the old Plymouth down
to feel alive again, to feel that rich
blood freight of summer,
the honeysuckle and hay weighing
the dew-cooled air on 41,
where there is only the fading moon,
its burden of ash and borrowed light
as he feels the world blowing right through him,
as if he wasn't there. . . .

Zeno Said

At 50, up Cold Springs Trail to Montecito Peak

Zeno said—though I have this second-hand—
that I'd never make it up this path.
But here I am,
more than half way to the sky,
fixed on a point but moving forward
despite his arrow across the stadium, half
of half way, ad infinitum.
So much
for theory in its thin apparel, its ready-to-wear.
So much, as well, for Someday, Maybe
and the Sweet By and By.
Three hours to the top,
legs burning, the angst of clouds
building in my lungs.
I wipe sweat
from my forehead, and watch little crowns of mist
evaporate from the oaks.
What was I thinking?
At this point, whoever looks for signs
and wonders will never get there. Jesus,
this is just dirt, and it comes to an end.
Even a little way up you can see that
whatever The Meek will inherit,
it's not this sparkling coast, not these haciendas
brazed with jacaranda and palm.
I have done the math,
the life by fractions—the heart counting its way
steadily out of the world.
I am unraveling
with the cow slip and morning glory,
with the star-blue ceanothus, my breath
coming short with the lisp of bay laurel and eucalyptus,
and by evening we are all unheard prayers.

Overhead, my old company of clouds, the respiration
of the dead suspended above their ardent bodies.

So much for the world,
I think they say.

At this height, I know the extravagance of air,
the unrestricted future falling away, the hung fire—
So much for detachment.
Even with the view
from the peak, what do we finally know
of ourselves, let alone the angels
who have gone about each dawn in their old coats,
a mist bright as wind through the oat straw
our only clue?
Only half the darkness
ever peels back from the earth,
and in these valleys and swales,
in the last shadows, you can still see that.

Now, I don't know what to ask for—
all the galaxies like nerve endings
in their bright net, pulsing,
and pulling back.
So much for the world
where the angels have lost something too,
or fallen from faith with the indecipherable
longing that supports the heavens.
The arithmetic of stars is beyond me,
the lost chalk of saints in the sky.

That poor soul, shivering in a trench coat,
living in the rusted truck by the trailhead,
his greasy arm in a greasy sling, making his forbidden fire
of twigs, tipping his green bottle up like a trumpet,
was silent, and disappeared behind the smoke
as we passed.
I'm sure from here
he's had a clear view to the sky each night,
to the bright mad head of the comet,
its white fizzy light like one lost wing,
like a smear of silver nitrate cauterizing the dark—
ten thousand years to the other side
and back. So much for time.

I doubt now
he expects much from a sky that apportioned
these various poverties here below.
I doubt
the abstract comforts of philosophy
have kept anything close to bitterness away.
Oh, that dream of the shadow of smoke—
so much for hope.
It's just memory
counting back, that desire to know, finally,
what it means to be here—I mean besides everything—
and from this mountain see the earth
curve out,
turning over and off into space,
and space itself seem nothing more
than a white dust over the parochial sea
where we were sure of the view once, by the Aegean.

Sure, there are things you can still pray for.
The clouds offer no argument against one realm
moving invisibly and without dissent at the edge
of another,
persuaded by the least suggestion
of wind in the manzanita to move beyond it all.
You can pray to be a cloud, I guess—
you can be that alone.
But I always hear
the voices of children in the trees,
and know there the incalculable velocity of loss,
where, above the town, I stood
in my cloud-white uniform shirt with stars
pasted on my collar, and sang songs in French
I'd learned by heart.
Now, as the light falls short,
I turn west for the diminuendo of starlight
rising on the blue scales of the past,
where everything has always been
floating perilously like candles in paper sacks
sent from the creek mouth out to sea.
So much for souls.

Haven't I had enough?
Not by half. Not even when I think
I've tempered grief and immediately
new points of pity fill in—hip pointer,
hamstring, bone spur, ventricular arrhythmic beat—
and I find myself settling for one dog-easy day,
just loose in the old streets on a Sunday,
ambling somewhere in the sun.
And that turns out to be no place,
finally, to recover anything—a few blocks
from the creek bed, and plastic grocery bags scuttle
through the new housing sites, one snagged
like some child's lost gown, in the high, thin boughs.

Hasn't the sky put up with our nonsense
all this time? Only half defeated by gravity,
why not pour what's left of your ambition
like a tablespoon of salt into the Pacific?

The avatars and ascended masters, I'm told,
sit in the silent altitudes with little to do,
despite snow and cloud banks that occlude a world
where community leaders take up resolutions
against the enervation of the grass,
where you can almost hear the lost anthems of elms
beyond the cul-de-sac.
The last mastodons
grew small and survived another twenty thousand years
on the channel islands. You're finally breathing
the blue pure air, crossing in the unqualified
direction of the light—so why question its glaze
igniting the date palms along the shore
like the stars that find their way
each night, clear across the sky?

for Charles Wright

Via Dolorosa—Santa Barbara, California

In those days there was more rain,
and though I stood often,
and very still, in the afternoons,
among the orange or lemon groves—
sun arriving, blooming in the water
beads on the deep waxy leaves—
no branches, in time, grew
from my arms, no blossoms
from my eyes so that I might
finally go back into the world
brilliant beyond longing.
I was transcendent only
until the dark came on
and the petitions of quail and towhees
quit along the lanes.

What it was I was forever
going to remember, I don't now know?
I went from one illuminated bough
to the next, to the sea bluff and
the Morse Code of clouds
as it revealed the vague intentions
in back of air.
                                        How will I ever know
again but to go half lost along
that road of losses—milk-white
heart, cup of thorns, mind
of blue fragments floating off
somewhere in search of the invisible. . . .

Out the one street, headed anywhere,
we drove after school in that
beaten bronze and beige Chevrolet,
past the dirt road and the hand-lettered
board saying Bam's Auto Court
with its half dozen trailers edging
the avocado trees, past the little
front street grammar school
and the Rexall Drug, long past the last dairy

and lemon grove that became the first
shopping mall and so said so long
to the '60s.
                    There was no allegory
in the wind. The past just blew away.
We all remember some different part
of the dust blowing up from a side street
and catching in the air as we let out
of the double feature at the California
Theater, looking up to god
knows what, straining
the galvanized daylight through our fingers
into our half-tranced eyes, checking
the clouds and roof tops, scuffing the soles
of our shoes on the sidewalk
to be sure, with the wind gusts,
that we were still there. . . .

God of Absence, God of markers
gone from the fields, God of tail pipes
and mufflers rusting on the roadside,
I pause here to pay respect, to turn
down the page of diminished fact,
to rattle bones so the soul holds on.

But what comfort was there
in the dwarf pine and mesquite,
who was there to pray over the last
mammoth dying under those icy stars
over the channel islands? The long ages
moved that far west, coming down
to a last under-sized example
adapted to its loneliness, isolated,
one day, by the melting sea. . . .
And the sea so beatific then,
translucent, green as a curling wave,
as a veil Michelangelo draped
over the Sibyl's shoulder
who revealed nothing
on the bright ceiling
of a sorrowful heaven—the way
of the past from which we are meant
to somehow again draw hope.

We stand before the sea again,
everything, it seems, already gone
before us—the consolations, the philosophies
like suits, like old coats to try on
in the Thrift; the religions
like the salvageable shoes shined up—
wingtips and brown & white spectators—
nearly gleaming in the greasy window.
And clouds of dust rising and falling
across the old west, the Oregon Trail,
El Camino Real.
                                        Still the sky somehow
clearer back there, still at its leisure
to follow a second thought through
the streets with the dying light
block to block, along the dim stations,
past the Carrillo Hotel, The Copper Coffee Pot,
The Fox Arlington. . . . The bruised evening
in the branches of the municipal trees
always at cross purposes in autumn
as I try to recall anything at all
about what I thought would come—
the salt breeze off the harbor, the little tune
at twilight that softly overcame the red tile roofs,
which I followed west along the sidewalks
where I was first alive, where stars lined up
to arrive with me, home by dark.

Lost Sky

sic transit gloria mundi
Mahon, Menorca

100 miles in any direction and
                                        the sky still has plenty
of time,
            and so is in no hurry to remember,
offer a clue
               as to which life this is. . . .

I'm sauntering along
                           in a fine straw hat, summer
trousers and shirt
                        the color of stones lining
the cart-wide streets,
                            anonymous against
the faded building sides,
                                where the canaries
and finches—set out in their twig cages
for the sun—and I
                          whistle pieces
of an aria beneath the unencumbered roofs,

thinking perhaps in terms of the heart,
of stones absolved by the sea. . . .

Winter is hardly anything
                                  here, a white
mid-day moon, a sliver of ice on the blue
is as close as it comes—
                               a wind
is serious every so often,
                                 the hills shrug
their shoulders beneath their old coats
of chamomile and fennel,
                                  each morning a mist
of acquiescence lifting out to sea. . . .
                                              And soon
the green shutters will close after the lunch hour,
late,
      and there, where a bright breeze breaks
off the bay
              igniting the high garden wall,

you turn once more to praise the loquats and gold
hibiscus,
     hands over your eyes like a prisoner
just released into the blinding light of noon. . . .

But now the linnets have abandoned the leafless
civic trees, their branches
             pointing every
which way above the horizon.
               4:00, the city dead
asleep, and you find yourself at the tables
in front of the American Bar,
               waiting reasonably,
as is the custom, for the waiter on duty
to stub his cigarette and set,
              reluctantly,
next to your folded Herald Tribune,
a glass of *fino*, as thinly amber
               as the coattails of daylight
trailing over the roof tiles
             to the west,
where, for a minute or two, all the old
theologies circle,
         like pigeons, like rings
of the elect to the sky—
            like the remedies of dust,
dispensed each day
          at this time from the stuffed pockets
of the rag man,
         shuffling alley to street, a man
of apparent contentment, who smiles and tips
his sun-bleached captain's hat
               each time
he sees you, god-knows-what in the sacks
on his creaking cart.
           You have half a dozen phrases
to fall back on—
         one for him in the afternoon,
and one for the newsstand,
              tabacalera, fish market
and the bar—
        one for the past you say to no one,
but that old high Latin
            will get you nowhere now—

not comfortably back down the burning

road to home,
or to Augustine's City of God, and who
would you recognize there,
though you speak,
beneath your breath to someone
beyond the shops,
someone not among the shopping crowds
soon drifting down the streets?
At 5:00 as the lights
snap on
across from you, only the usual
ghosts of the evening hour return—
sparrows the color
of October, chorusing in praise
of the constellations,
the offerings of crumbs
wind -blown on the chairs
and ground . . .
and in the pines at sunset,
that region
of memory
dimming once again with a longing
for something
as indeterminate as the lattice-work of clouds,
a plume
of black smoke dissolving
into the last striations
of the blue,
as it exhales through your bones and skin
and you begin again
the little poem of the soul, recalling the lines
for the spirit
at last content somewhere, floating
through the streets
aimed no higher finally than the sugared light,
sparkling
in the bakery windows—
steam,
bright thread rising,
unraveling
through the increasingly familiar dark.

Mediterranean Clouds—Es Castell, Menorca

> The Big Empty is also a subject of some note,
> Dark, dark and never again . . .
> —Charles Wright

Clouds on a string in the west,
spelling out
their blank predicament,
marshalling no argument
against the dark
we're headed for.
Bits of Styrofoam
bob on the swells,
the sun
shakes out its dreams in dust
and was dreaming
of dust all along. . . .
We've read the certifications
of the dead,
we've made our calculations in the air
and turned
out here before the waves
with little more
than the detachment,
the blandishments of daylight
grazing our cheeks.
Earlier each day
the sky calls in its debts,
the insolvency of our hearts—
the fog unspools,
so this can't help but be another poem
about the soul. . . .

Outside Bar Miramar, on the *Calla Fonts,*
you sit
with an *Estrella,* you sit with your life
like the light blue
spaces shifting off with the apostasy
of dusk,
with crumbs blowing off the plate
of bread and oil
and olives.
You watch the jumping fish rise

out of the bay,
the first edge of moon,
both silver. . .
you accept these
compensations,
the small salvations
of late afternoon, the fair weather
clouds reflecting
the comparative poverties
of the past, tattered shirts
on a rooftop line. . . .
But this is the new life
of the spirit—
shopping for wine or onions,
a potato omelet
in the bar by the bay.

Let the stars starve in the dark
with their bright hexagrams
and prescience,
their persistence after death
with or without us. . . .
At the mouth of the harbor
the buoy lights
set against the sky
might be stars
just as well.

Sit with me by the pittosporum and marguerites
and think—
St. Augustine came to aggravate us
with sin
and our simple desire
for the earth,
to remind us about the soul
and the unreliable
veil of the senses,
and offered that we should not
expect evidence
for what is beyond
us in the first place.
Long before the stars
or galaxies,
the universe held the lightless seed

of our every atom,
unbreathing and flat, without
dreams.
And before that, what?
What bright threads
up the long stem of the dark?
What resemblance
might instruct us?
Sunset, and St. Augustine
is peeling an orange,
and the tiny spray of acid
breaking from the peel
gives off the brilliance
of the Spanish coast
burning above Valencia,
of the world
he has defamed,
having grown old in it.
The light
of this world surely is the light
of the other. . . .

The sun's burden settles
on palm leaves
feathered out
by an inconsequential wind . . .
nothing stands
in place of the world,
although Byzantine
mystic Nicophorus the Solitary
told us, "Attention
is the appeal of the soul to itself."
though the palms
gaze indifferently out to sea,
though there is no escaping
the stars.

In your notebook, you again take up the passage
about the passing
and glory of the world—
(you've kept track—
more passing than glory).
The sparrows await more
crumbs and do not commiserate

about mortality—
in the chair across from you, you have
the soft light of October
and the little schismatics
in their cheerful waistcoats
do not put one day
before another,
do not find the handiwork
of the infinite in clouds.
It's all you need to breathe
out with evening and accept
your inconsequence
among the thistles and fennel.
Never mind
the circumstantial accounts,
the refined grist of scholarship—
the theory
never the thing itself.
The field larks sing
for the sky,
the preamble
of light tumbling
in their blood,
still in their pebble-sized hearts.
Brush strokes on the horizon,
the imponderable
backdrop of air.
The birds suggest,
it is impudent to question
what we're given
before the dark,
what thin intimations spin away
just over our heads—
what clues dissolve against the blue,
or just hold vaguely on,
like a little mist, almost overlooked,
and offered up
on the salt-white light
off the sea. . . .

Poem Freely Accepted from the Polish

In the old masters' landscape
the trees have roots beneath
the oil paint . . . — Wislawa Szymborska

We are not so badly off if we can
Admire Dutch Painting. . . .

. . . those trees outside the window, which probably exist . . .
— Czeslaw Milosz

We could do worse than walk through the representational
world, praising the common daylight

the least of us deserves—or its lucid and frank
enunciation in pen and ink with

objective air and space for the trees of the old world
to come to order beside the cornfield

and river, beneath a horizon brazed, frayed with grist,
the progress of a windmill or two

dissolving into afternoon, a linen-colored sail
up stream. How much could it hurt

to admire the unacknowledged principles of trees,
their metaphorical fortitudes upheld?

And couldn't it well be Philips Koninck himself,
the obscure Dutch artist, pausing

on the path there to pencil himself in forever, nothing
at that moment more important

than the little hymn of dust seasoning everything
on our behalf, setting the world

forth in a brown wash—and in his black hat and habit
appraising the elms around Rotterdam

set against the defeated landscape, thin-winged against
the sky as they easily outlive us. . . .

In Kew Gardens it was clear that they outshine us—
cedar of Lebanon, green as the deep sea's

dream, slick with the pewter sun, 235 years already
matriculated in the blue, and no worries

yet—the ash and false acacia, atlas cedar in its jade-
bristle sheen. Where beyond the present

did I suppose I was going that morning the rain
arrived with its brief memoranda and

a thousand small reproaches for idleness, the dull silt
of over-contemplation? Whatever

I thought I was called to do was no clearer than
the dusty windshield, the *basso profundo*

of the ocean and fog, grey fish bumping in the tides.
I think God knows I'm not kidding around

anymore, no matter what useless things I've prayed for
or praised—I should be satisfied

with all the cilia of light just stirring back and forth,
up from unlit roots to the feathery arms,

even the white cactus flowers breaking out like
the tide on the night sea to briefly defy

the old saying—*Darkness, Darkness*—covering
the borderlands of memory where we

already had everything we would ever need, where
so many leaves cover the ground. . . .

And that sense of hope? It was replaced with middle age—
with a realistic longing for something

you can no longer name in your bones. The sky
overlooking us with our unfulfilled

fable where the first one on the Neolithic plain
holds up a rock, or fire in his hand

to defend a few ferns and poplars at the edge of a pool
or field, where grain was scattered

unspecified as the stars, where we beheld the great
bodies of the great beasts in blood

and berry juice, in charcoal and sulfur on the cold
cave walls. Once we wanted so little

from the light and were appeased with our inelegant
equations in the night, with our simple

misunderstanding of the relative theories, the special
interests in the universe. We had faith

in the invisible litany of oak leaves, smoke in wind,
the starry Sanskrit of an older firmament,

the fragrance of mint or coriander winding through
the halls. I will not pray against

the vicissitudes again, whatever they might be, however
many more steps into the air. . . .

In the yard this morning a gold finch and great
western grackle in the bottlebrush,

a scarlet tanager with his brick red head and road sign
yellow and black, perusing the blooming

jacaranda, the dust-gold silk tree. We will lean out
a long time toward the sun, with the sea

cataloguing the green past, with our coats on hangers,
with our slouch like clouds billowing

in the shoulders, of course, and the eucalyptus grove
in sepia, the amber leaves, the fall

air rusting, the afternoon rich with the apprehensions
of death in the castor bean. We will rise

or fall within easy sight of the angels, and it will
surprise no one now when I say

I have no new feelings about God who I no longer
believe is hiding above the golden

sycamores as I did as a boy, netting shining tadpoles
in the creek and placing them in a jar

to release another day. All things said and done,
I feel as if all things might well be

said and done. But here I am taking in the air
in the park above the cliffs again,

more or less equivalent to the trees, reading our
best poets, realizing I've not had two

original bits of wisdom on all those slips of paper
stuffed in one coat pocket or another.

This is not modesty. These days, even an old song
on the radio can wreck your heart.

Sunlight shifts through the boughs as you begin
to turn over what-in-the-world

it's added up to all this time? And even with dust
in your mouth, you have fifty ways

to say, I fear death more than most, and have hidden
it among the breathing leaves,

or wrapped it in the breakers along the shore in return
for nothing. This is not philosophy—

my blood tastes of the sea, the salt of the white ash
        of time and light going forward, heartless

in a few lines. Somewhere toward the back, I've been
        content singing my small devotion

to light, and to the birds that carry their part of it
        through the sky, and who hasn't

thought of that? And how much do the trees really ask
        of us after all? I hold my arms out,

reading my book, like the rest seated before the concert
        and string arrangements of the leaves.

So long at the level of the trees—a poem seeming another
        instance of unaccomplished love.

Five Days Rain

"Just keep thinkin' Butch, that's what you're good at."
—The Sundance Kid

"The NOW in Chaos Theory is the phase transition state where all choices are open."
—Judy Petree's Home page on Chaos Theory

Another cloudburst afternoon with the old sky,
the new sky, washing away. . . .

Still years from retirement, but I'm thinking
of the life I might have had

as a theoretical physicist . . . except the background,
some facility in math & science,

I had everything it takes . . . forget the sheets of rain
falling like a shredded Bible, the past,

the leaves choking the drainpipes, so many soggy facts.
I need to understand the sea's

soft heart, its galactic equilibrium—I've been the dreamer
who's seen it shining effortlessly

beyond death, beyond the as yet unseen particles
and additional dimensions.

The universe is conceivably a horseshoe, a flip-flop or
knot of strings, a loop-de-loop, a mesh

of time riding blind on its own back—I could
have come up with that, no sweat.

Einstein daily thought his way out of his socks,
usually got it right the first time

with gravity and the big laws of light, and didn't
even show all his work. He kept

the unadorned formula for matter on a scrap
in his vest pocket, next to his pipe,

and though he never saw himself as a troubadour
heading out alone to sea in a boat,

a breeze in his spindrift hair, he valued the fanciful
assumptions of our blood,

and the math came together, glimmering like the 1950s
starlight in Rosemary Clooney's eyes.

A clear vision of sorts was possible, even beside
the incautious sea, the relapse of waves.

Now they've slowed the speed of light with a deeper than
deep-freeze freeze; and the physics

all fail once things get smaller than an atom, but who's
going there? Who needs neutrinos?

They pass right through us, attached to nothing—
expendable extras discarded

a few seconds after it all really got going. It seems
you make it up as you go, and

none of us here long enough to prove things otherwise.
Nonetheless, I think this is where

my talents truly lie—all the rain adding up to
the invisible, pulling drops along,

down to us, into earth, angels descending a glass
ladder, dissolving into thin air. . . .

Here, the low mountains rise into clouds, clouds
I've seen arranged like pillows

beneath the bare feet of saints as they lifted off
from the world in their grey robes,

no longer weighed down by their molecules, and
we're to take it all on faith. And so

it's the theory of emptiness that concerns me,
    where the mind goes in the end

when it's no longer even dust? Once I stood at
    Punta Prima, salt spray and wind,

asking something predictably momentous of the sea,
    and it rolled on in its indolence

and uncertainty, and so I had my vast answer
    and strolled the emptied streets

in Menorca—everyone else dozing, or smoking
    on the sofa after lunch—

and discovered there the spatters of light, the solar
    splendor of oil-glazed puddles

in the stone, which was gone in a breath, like pigeons
    scattered by the backfire of a car.

In the square I waited for evening, for the pictograms,
    the anarchy of the stars to argue

one way or another across the drab grids of the mind—
    shimmering like the old tales

of Paradise. No one is listening any more. I find my cats
    swirled like grey constellations

on the bed, and, as they sleep, catch myself talking
    out loud to them about the world

losing faith with itself all around us. No matter,
    I imagine it's still the same over Paris,

uncomplicated nostalgia of rain clouds drifting above
    the boulevards, and the lives passing

through there as if through one grand Gare de Lyon,
    every filigree of wind and sun-polished

mansard roof in frescoes on the water-blue walls,
    a great gold clock whirring overhead,

angels from the 18th century riding the golden crest
    of cloud, looking no further than

Montparnasse, all of us staring up at the same sky above—
    so much utter confusion, releasing

for that moment, like pollen from the trees, like rain
    back to its ultimately unseeable source.

My Parents' Photographs

Who knew I looked like Pablo Neruda
in 1948, years before he'd look like that?
But in one of my parents' baby pictures,
above the Pacific and Humboldt Bay,
bald as a pope, or wearing that same cap
he'd later wear, I do—I'm propped up on
the hood of their cloud-colored Pontiac,
arms spread out to each side as if
blessing the air, learning my balance
for the years of surfing to come, or
wondering what my chances were of
lifting off into the rising wind with
the few syllables at my command, with
a wide-eyed and under-exposed joy.

Here's a boy, his happy hair slicked
back with Wildroot Cream Oil in 1952.
His mother and Aunt have taken him
to the Cincinnati Zoo; he's oblivious
to his matching home-made floral
shirt and shorts, his ridiculous white
as Ivory Soap Flakes, Hollywood sun-
glasses. And for no apparent reason,
he's still grinning out of the grey
light of this wallet-sized snap.

Already now, I am old enough
for my mother to be passing on
her photos—a practical matter,
I suppose, as, nearing 80, there's
no one else . . . but how do you
look past the light dissolving
at the corners, the black &
white despair that has gathered
all this time like the dull and
distant clouds in the corner

of this one above her childhood
farmhouse? A book of absence,
the specific gravity of loss.

Among them her umber, studio-
softened portrait—an RN during
the war—bangs like Bette Davis,
a flip like a dozen other stars;
it was auburn, as they said then.
And how young and harmless
she and my father both look
in color Christmas cards with me
and our Irish Setter, there on
Miramar beach before everyone
had heard about Santa Barbara,
and anyone could live there.

Before that we'd moved east when my father
finished school and found a job. In this one,
I'm 3, and despite a grey West Virginia January
afternoon, and to escape our dingy apartment
a few blocks from the decent one my father
was refused because he had a child—(though
he looked the woman straight in the face and
offered to drive to the river, drown the child,
and return in 15 minutes)—I'm outside, posed
on the cement steps beside my birthday cake.
My father unfolds the Kodak and shoots as I
sit still as the part in my hair. I look pleased
though I'm in a raincoat that comes to my knees
and wearing stiff white leather toddler shoes,
because the cake is big with white Crisco
frosting and red sugar roses—pleased when
my father calls me "Crisco," though it's grey
and grainy all about us in this 8 x 10, where
my coat and cap and I match the grizzled
atmosphere of Charleston. For what it's worth,
I have yet to begin looking up to the sky.

And I'm happy for one the size of 4 postage stamps,

taken inside the farm house . . . I can barely see to
climb into that wedge of light in my grandfather's lap
as he sits in his Morris Recliner, in his tan Dickey
shirt and trousers, his retired farmer's uniform.
I am 2 or 3, wearing shorts, sheared for summer,
and so our half-bald heads shine together. Then
one I never saw—grandfather and grandmother standing
alone on a Florida beach, late '40s, early '50s;
he's wearing a dark pin-striped suit and Panama hat;
she's in a flowered dress, in high black lace shoes,
pressing a modest bonnet with one hand to her head.
They've been to church or out to Sunday supper, as
dressed up as they will ever be. They are floating,
surrounded by an amber haze, the beach stretches
away in a cloud . . . I think I see a dusting of flour
on her cheek—she pulls the stool up to the kitchen
counter and hands me a water glass so I can press
biscuits, white as sea light, from the dough. . . .

My father's are sadder . . . for the blur and rusty
pallor from his mother's time, the stiff Edwardian
posing with her sister turn of the century—1900—
the one no one cares about any more. My father, 3
in this '20s sepia haze with ivory borders, wears
a pith helmet and uncharacteristic grin in the jungle
of backyard Ohio. Here's my grandfather Lon with my
waif-like father in their '30s caps and knickerbockers
at Niagra Falls, a once-in-a-lifetime opportunity, a place
I only saw on boxes of '50s Shredded Wheat. Or several
of the columns and two-story imperial high school.
And beneath the ionic capitals, I barely recognize
my father in his graduation gown and mortar board,
the modest scholar he would never really become.

Then in an air cadet uniform, outbreak of the war,
all that small town significance—all of our relatives
soon gone—Uncle Charlie who lived in a hotel, and
Bernie who drove by each night for beer, Aunt Babe,
straw-thin in her bones even then—on the cement
porch of the big house you could buy back then for

a handshake and a few dollars down in the middle
of America, in a place like Washington Court House,
Ohio. Flip forward 50 years, after my father's death,
I'm handed a box with photos and an empty billfold,
and there is one packet from the drug store, labeled
in ball point pen, simply "home." No relatives, none
of my grandparents or their white slat-board house,
no statues, street signs or faithful dogs, but just color

print after color print of the town in the first glories
of autumn, the town he came back to only once, late,
I think, in the '70s. He took the train cross-country,
having stepped off a plane state-side after the war,
having piloted DC-3s Cairo to Brazil, re-fueling in
the south Atlantic, on that dot of rock, Ascension Island,
having lost his only friend in the world, Howard, on his
last day as a flight instructor. He vowed never to get in
a plane again—not to go home, not to see his mother alive
or dead. But that last visit, took his last snaps around
the town, the blazing gold and burnt sienna, the crimson

rush of leaves and air, of parks, the Indian burial
mounds all in Kodachrome prints—trees everywhere
as in that vanished garden you carry with you always,
no matter where you live . . . . No people, just that
burning past living in softened Technicolor where
you most likely will never go again. All these things
so fixed and heavy with light, and gone, that wreck
your heart and never save you in the end. Packets
of the past you pass along to children, if you have
children, and if not, put away and try to not,
with the dark inching closer, ever look at again. . . .

I don't know what to make of a dream
the other night—my father kissing me
on the cheek as he never did in life,
not decked-out in the coffee-colored suit
and knit tie of his spiffy college snaps.
For his penance, I suppose, he has to wear
shabby clothes from some metaphysical

Thrift—trousers cuffed too short, tattered
coat, padding leaking out the shoulder
seam so perhaps he might know,

learn at last what mattered here, if far
too late for the little left in an envelope
of prints. All of it so long ago, and yet
by some accounts, no more than a blink
or two of light passing through the earth.
Whatever the coordinates of loss—dreams,
3 x 5s, 8 x 10s, sun-glint on the sea—each
image we hold up is an enlarged silence,
cloud forms, ashes shifting, losing shape—
a coincidence of the light we briefly were.

Eternity

(being a condensed spiritual and aesthetic biography)

for Virgil Suarez

No one says I look 55— no one says I don't, except my new friend Virgil. He has two catholic daughters and like me, hates to fly, but there's no other way to get home in time for the youngest's lst Communion. I almost remember mine. . . I've been scared ever since—of Death, of course. You tell me why . . . . In 2nd grade, the nun lectured us about Eternity, which almost arrived later from Cuba in the early '60s, Cuba where my friend Virgil was born, which has at least one entrance to hell and exits in Spain and L.A. In the afterlife, I don't think anyone is rolling cigars while someone reads them Don Quixote in the original. Anyway, we were going to spend Eternity in hell if we did not do as we were told. Sister explained that Eternity was like an enormous steel ball, the size of the earth, upon which an eagle, gliding in from the cosmic starry dark beyond Cleveland and the east coast, once every million years, landed and took off again. The time it took that steel ball to completely wear away from the friction of the eagle landing and lifting away was less than a second of Eternity, the time we'd be burning on a hot rock for cussing, eating hot dogs on Fridays, not making our yearly Easter obligation of communion and mass, or having impure thoughts about Belinda Sanchez. Go figure.

What if, on the practical side, the universe—and so time-space—does curve back on itself like a huge quesadilla? We're going nowhere. What, then, have we been suffering for all along? More specifically, what have I been doing with that image like a fish hook in my brain for 48 years? Nuns, with their psycho-spiritual hammer-locks, were terrorists, and they did not discriminate among ages or ethnic groups. Death, darkness, and sure damnation were there equally for us all if we didn't stop talking during mass and go out and finagle quarters from relatives and folks on our block for the pagan babies. Dear God. I don't know what angel brings me these lines in the middle of the night after I'm up and down the hall to the bathroom, brings them every few years like a palm tree and a pool of water appearing after sands have shifted for no reason, like some metaphysical crust of light. Some angel sweeping down with dust, one in the back of the chorus singing hosannas like nobody's business who has a little time to spare, an angel who every now and then hands off a few imagistic granules while I'm flaming away here in the flesh, in darkness where I might not know the source but would know a gift when I heard one.

Once I'm half awake and the cells are ticking over like new stars, I lose track of time and switch the lamp on and off and write down phrases, losing sleep—what does it come to? The door of a '59 Chevy swings open like a vault and lets out some earlier, more sprightly version of me, only a few blocks from happiness, or the sea, which ever comes first—with my papers and a new poem in hand—more than I arrived with. Who knew where I was headed? The nuns were sure: Hell. Virgil and I voted for Spain, even southern California if that's the best we could do to breathe cool salt air. Maybe I could do this forever, who knows? As I was taught, worse things could happen to me. Outside of Time, will poems matter? Why ask now—I'm not an academic, an administrator, slick in a Republican suit. We're not for long, not forever. Death, of course. And next? I hope it's not hell, or anywhere near Pennsylvania, where I already served ten years for my sins.

Dear God. Thank you for the gift of the eccentric brain, this associative jelly. Thank you for this moonraking poem which keeps me alive in prayer, in doubt, and in hope. This poem which for once did not take 5 months and 50 drafts, though I would have waited patiently as always—like salt dissolving from the sea, like air gathering to be somewhere else, like the last flake of rust outside of time . . . .

Buckley y yo

Asi mi vida es una fuga y todo lo pierdo y todo es del olvido, o del otro, / thus my life is a fugue and I lose everything and everything belongs to oblivion or to the other one

—Jorge Luis Borges, *"Borges y yo"*

Fugue, or Fugue state, is a dissociative disorder characterized by reversible amnesia for personal identity, including the memories, personality, and other identifying characteristics of individuality.

It's the other guy, the one who picks up the checks, who knows someone in New York, who's at his desk all day, working like a mule driver. I spend afternoons in the park, reading a little philosophy, a bit of pre-digested astrophysics, an occasional Italian mystery novel, though no one stops to ask if gravity waves have arrived, or inquires about the best or surest way to proceed in life? Still, it's good, someone said, to have a job—no doubt one of those mule drivers. . . .

It's the sacks of small potatoes that have me talking to myself—something's better than nothing one of us is sure to say. You've always believed you knew what you were doing, but *viejo*, this far down the road, how many books does it take to make sense of things? That pebble that clicked against the office window—did it fall from the beak of a bird, or was it lifted from an empty field by wind and dismissed by the blue? Did it travel millions of miles from the icy Kuiper Belt at the edge of the solar system just to get your attention for a second so you'd stop brooding about Time?

I vote we stop running around reading verses, pretending to be someone. Let's throw our hands up and admit we're ice and dust, some atoms fobbed off by a star even God has forgotten, get in some R & R. Despite what our man Einstein said, it sure looks like we're just a random roll of the interstellar dice, a happy coincidence of atoms which look to be less than 5% of the universe, of the whole shootin'-match, as they used to say. . . . It looks to me like we're lucky there's so much as a harmonica wheezing somewhere in all this darkness, let alone that Gustav Holst wrote for orchestra, choir, opera, ballet, *and* the planets—excepting Earth, where we stand at the shore of infinite waters, and Pluto that's been cast back into the frozen junk pile circling in the night for nothing.

But has cosmology ever boosted sales? A couple hundred people might pick up your book, but that's nothing before God, the accountant, or even before the dead—a large percentage of whom still contribute to that 5%. So you might listen to your relatives and write that self-help Western, or a home-improvement Mystery even though we both know Pessoa said, "The only mystery is there being people who think about mystery." You buy that? Think about the Harris tweed found in the Thrift that fit as if it were tailored for you, or me. That's 1,000 to 1 against intelligent design. When fog rolls in there will be plenty of time to walk the cliff path wearing that coat and an old fedora, recalling those '50s black & white British films in which wandering about was a respected profession. Pessoa—who had five people talking interestingly enough in his head, one after the other—also admonished: "To think of God is to disobey God." Does that clear it up?

And that young man interviewing you for the *Gazette,* with questions about your early work, the theory behind all you've lost—you're doing a lot of tap-dancing to get around looking like just another *pazzo* sitting by the edge of the sea. Jesus, who thought we'd ever have "early work"? It's one thing to point to an influence, it's another to give the money back.

How are we ever going to travel fast enough to slow down Time, that black well of energy pushing the planet out to the edges of who-knows-what, faster each year? As the glittery facts play out, they're just metaphors for speculation, for more pages—perhaps that's what keeps you going? But I see through you, *compadre;* you'd have written fewer of those home-sick odes if you really knew what was up. Wander your streets and parks and perhaps then you'll be content to let someone else try to explain the muddled dialogue between ourselves and the eucalyptus—the molecular idiom, the one-sided explication of the clouds vis-à-vis your most recent representation for the soul?

The way I see it, I'm the thin one with all his hair, still hanging out at the beach in his 20s, posing by the palms with a copy of *War and Peace,* trying to look intelligent, blissful without a savings account or publications. You're still afraid to face me at the card table, the stars looking over your shoulder. Shut up and deal—7-card no-peek-roll-your-own. Poetry and philosophy will save themselves.

Why don't you copy out the recipe for Spaghetti Arrabiata—you'll feel like someone just pronouncing it, and following the instructions will, no doubt, remind you of String Theory—who else might, in some parallel universe, be doing all the preparation so one of us can lean back and light up a *Partagas,* the smoke swirling off toward that asteroid belt. Time and Eternity were concocted on earth.

Borges said his life was a fugue, and he wasn't talking song and dance; he meant half of him wanted a peaceful un-famous life free of ambition. Forget your notebooks and fabulous fountain pens, the alleged transcendental trail of crumbs. You can't argue that the stars are within our reach, even if I'm standing on your shoulders, or vice-versa. If there is a conscious state beyond the stars, what's the chance we'll remember our former restless selves?

Against Flying

Wind pushing Italian cypress side to side,
          bougainvillea spattered
against the bone-colored wall, the high,
          mad heads of eucalyptus
beating the air . . . in a few days, my step-
          mother, who has moved
to New Mexico on Social Security and a shoestring—
          Social Security which is a shoestring—
who drove a U-haul all the way, will be 71, will have
          no hope beyond the sky.

For Christmas she sends a wrinkled teak-colored
          photograph of my father
from the '40s, impossibly young on the tarmac
          in his Air Cadet leather jacket,
in pleated, loose-fit, trousers. He's wearing
          high topped tennis shoes,
foot set confidently on the tire of his trainer—
          a light, single-engine job
that looks like it could barely dust a cabbage field.
          But he's sure he's prepared
for life, he's got his game-face on—as we say now—
          for the photo, as if to tell
Lon and Eva he's in control and knows where
          he's heading, knows what
the world should be, what it all will come to.
          In this, he never changed.

65 years ago, he was banking turns, slip-streaming
          the wide, lace-curtain blue—
a world on its way out. He was smiling probably,
          easy with his airy calisthenics,
a few bars of "Skylark" looping through his head.
          He was crewing with Howard,
his only friend lifelong, another boy from Washington
          Court House, Ohio—Howard
who finished up as a flight instructor, who made it
          until the last day of the war
when a student flew them straight into the ground.

My father landed state-side
and never set foot in a plane again, not even to go
home 40 years later for
his mother's funeral, though he took the train once
to New York City and Broadway
to see "The Music Man" and "Oklahoma" alone—
that world he remembered
and thought he'd saved, by God, for good.

A moon in a buttermilk sky, but no one's thinking
of Hoagy Carmichael anymore.
That sky is gone and that moon, and the stardust
that fell for years after the war.
There's an empty bench on the campus of Indiana U.
where the simple '50s died,
where no one spends the lonely nights, or wonders, sometimes,
anymore. Certainly it's not the moon
he saw swelling over Abadan, over hotels and Supper Clubs
in Cairo, whistling a Cole Porter tune,
walking the streets, tapping his gazelle bone cane,
growing a beard that had him
looking like a Babylonian, one of the winged beasts guarding
the gates of Nineveh. But it's
the only moon I'll ever see, glimmering in a wine glass,
another year dissipating, as I am
less and less sure of anything except the undeniable
solitude of the air all around us,
heavy as I am with all the days flown away, days when
I was trying to make a life
out of nothing much but poems, wondering if I shouldn't be
studying Law, or Real Estate
to combat high rents, ads for scientifically advanced
vacuum cleaners, hair transplants,
frequent flyer miles to Hawaii or Rome—or hedging
my bets with the Weekend Warriors
in the National Guard? How comfortable it seems now,
all that trouble and turbulence,
long miles past the days when success was just ducking
the draft and Vietnam another semester.
Locke and Kierkegaard aside, we faced immediate loss
and rewards, the stock exchange
of our lives in that first Lottery where a # below 285

meant you'd be running through
the jungle—safer logging a million miles in a plane.

I look again at my father—1940? 41?—
he knew as much then as all the rest of them who knew
it all and dropped bombs on Dresden,
who took to the skies with hell fire and tracers on their tails,
flew DC 3s Egypt to S. America,
the whole world literally in front of them. What was there
a man couldn't learn? Not to jump
in planes and fly foreign skies, not to re-up, push your luck,
roll the bones with death,
the grand prize a washer/dryer and built-ins in Levittown?

Every few years, to get to England
with my wife, I combine enough Rx and cocktails to float
a boat of neurotics, and come out
level, just a close shave past calm when we land. I no longer
get on planes to go read my poems
for 40 minutes to 35 people—this late in the proceedings,
what will it change? An audience
of crows will do, alighting each evening atop the pines,
exchanging a clattering camaraderie,
endorsing, as I and my friends used to, the dusk suspended
above the dark assimilation
of their wings. I'm always looking at the sky, its deep blue
silence still one-sided, no matter
how many assumptions we hurl up there. "My Stars!"
my father's mother used to exclaim,
but they're no one's. And even if my heart sometimes
overlooks the fact that we fell
from comets, from sprays of interstellar dust, odds are,
with all the sand in our shoes,
we are little more than the discards of the wind.

M Theory and The Apothegm of Bones

Realize Jesus warned you.
Realize you are being lied to . . .
—Dennis Saleh

Yes, that was me in my 20s, believing in reincarnation, thinking anything
could happen next. I had my cards read, and in my last life I was,
she said, a lesser king of France . . . but the dream
that kept repeating all through

my teenage years insisted I was machine-gunned escaping a compound
during WW II. Even now, it's not damp or cold that the small
of my back doesn't feel drilled with it . . . but even if
I still might believe, I hope I'm wrong.

The prophet Ezekiel visited a valley full of dry bones and brought them
to life simply by mentioning the name of the Lord. How long
exactly was eternity? I got the general idea sitting
through 16 years of religion classes. . . .

And this is where the Buddha and every Yogananda come out ahead—
any individual can sit quietly and accept the enlightenment
of the trees, see the soul in apposition to the clouds,
or not—a little humming may help you

compose yourself. I last saw Allen Ginsberg at the Dodge Festival, alone
in the tent, eating his lunch. Too embarrassed to go up to him,
my wife went over and asked if he'd sign our book;
he obliged, then quietly went back

to his sandwich, knowing it was likely a matter of so many more sandwiches,
the improbability of paradise having increased over time vis-à-vis
the trigonometry of the void, the cosign of the dark,
the ineluctable ellipses of doubt. . . .

Regardless, I keep looking up to the night sky, overbite of the Milky Way,
each star clambering over all the others, never enough to fill
the heart. What reason is there to believe someone
up there likes me? 60 years bobbing

and weaving, taking celestial rabbit punches, ducking, keeping my head down
to avoid the knockout combination, and I never come out ahead
on points—the fix is in, as I've long suspected. Even when
I was 8 I didn't believe Doris Day singing

"*Que Sera, Sera.*" I knew Fate was a sucker-punch. I liked The Harmonicats
playing "Peg 'O My Heart" for Pete's sake—a nostalgia for what
I had no idea? Half the time, I was just a sentimental kid.
And though in dance class I'd got

the Cha-Cha down pat, there was science, Johannes Kepler and his Music
of the Spheres, beatific physics, unheard harmonics that invisibly
held each heavenly body in place. Sure, now they have it
right—the new theory with 11 dimensions

filling out the elegant equation, and more strings attached. Who wants to go
there? Multiple universes, Time before Time? Go figure. Anyway,
a switch was thrown, and the grand unified field theory
went to pieces all around us, which is why

gravity is just weak enough to let us run the bases, but rarely hit it out of the park,
so loosely connected to the electromagnetic force that it must account
for the National League losing the All Star Game12 years
in a row. You think it over, you write about it—

but how in the world are you sure this is what you should be doing, that this is
worth a life? What's next, what's behind door # 3? In his 90s Michelangelo
despaired of all his art—great art—had it been as important
as finding that starry gate to God? If you ask that

question, you already have your answer. I knew every road in Montecito by 12,
on my bike, in my dreams, went blind a time or two driving the Freeways
in San Diego before I cut back on the hard stuff. And Yes,
I think there was a light in my eyes. . . .

Like my father, I killed one rabbit and gave up hunting for good. I don't know
how I ever learned anything. And I don't believe in eternal damnation—
especially for stealing candy bars, or eating flank steak on Friday—
but I'm more than ready to make an exception

for couple of colleagues. And in the '70s I was worrying too much about the rent
to support the Sandinistas. The Incas slid off the metaphysical agenda
long ago and were done in by an insider deal with Pizarro—
so what were our chances? How far back

does it go? Do I believe it's likely we'll come up a nose short on the transcendental
exacta? You bet—dollars to donuts—cosmic puts and options, loop holes
in the stellar fine print, knot to knot of light and matter,
because we like to have a choice.

But, close enough to the Exit now, I believe I could give God another chance—
you never know your luck. One membrane in the middle of nowhere
rubs up against another and, Bang, a big roll of the bones and
you have all the atoms you'll ever need. . . .

Thank You Note: Recent Technological & Cosmological Musings

Lamp out, window open to the stars—I'm ready
    to say good night, but not for good . . .
I'm nowhere near the bottom of my list of complaints.
    Nevertheless, thorny as I've grown,
some gratitude is overdue for having made it this far,
    so many sands slipping through
the untraceable fingers of the void. So Thank You
    for the wingspan of my lungs
that allows me to hover here, that daily propelled me
    over the dusty paths I ran
through childhood on— no blessing brighter
    than breath for which
we should further beseech the balconies of the sky,
    or whichever cloud it is
You watch from in the disguises of matter or light.

    Each afternoon in our backyard—
as I suppose You know—towhees and tufted tit mice
    praise the bounty of sun flower seeds
my wife sets out. They recognize her, and even
    the red faced finch sings to shame us
all for the little that falls to him. And Thank You
    for the Italian cypresses where
the finches' flats stack into the air, where they
    appear morning and evening for
their arias like Cavaradossi praising the starlight
    he is soon to lose, or become,
putting all his heart into it, like the birds. Thank you
    for softening my heart so I could
love Puccini's splendor and despair, for surviving
    my stupid youth, in which I
called it Strangle the Cat in Costumes Music . . .
    I pretty much knew everything then,
all of it coming to a boil in my blood, insinuating
    that I'd live forever—all that buzzing
like neon in my veins. Thank you for letting me
    realize one clear thing, if only
the darkness before us at last—finally, what is
    more mystical than the night

where less and less is hidden from us any more?
Well, the number of universes
out there is still up for debate, and where exactly
this one ends and what's
on the other side has been argued to distraction,
or, as the lady told
Bertram Russell, "It's turtles, all the way down."
You worked it all out
Before taking the rest of eternity off, bored
with the eons around you
falling away like star dust, cosmic talc . . . .
Similarly, a little shine's
gone off particle physics as it's pretty much done
with us, here taking
advantage of a limited-time-offer and no warrantee.
But Thank You
for letting us at least pick up on the relative distances
that always exceed us—
it gives us something to focus on besides Supporting
Our Troops, something
in our age to stimulate the jellied synapses before
they dry out completely
as the clay they came from, a little filigree to lobby
on our long-term behalf,
to apply about the edge of our entreaties, to my
speculation clanking
daily about my brain like loose change in a jar.

I've never sent a Text Message—
is there another kind? The meaning of our information
always seemed the point,
and soon enough we'll all arrive at that point
where all roads meet,
no matter what theories or manner of hosannas
we've sent up, electronically
or on scrolls in cracked jars, print-outs or not.
To be on the safe side,
to play the house odds, I'll add a Thank You for this
quiet awning of shade,
the hours left to look out above the hills and only
think about what is out
above the hills; for holding off the rush of technology

    until I was too old to care
about smart phones or nanoseconds. I would rather
    take my time putting it
down in some sky-blue loops and scrawls with my
    fountain pen that still flows
with its tenuous possibilities despite being dipped
    in a last dark well of hope.

A Little About Not Knowing Very Much

When I was 5 and first in school,
I refused, after lunch each day,
to take a nap, fearing
there was nothing
on the other side
of sleep.
            It was something
I arrived with on the planet,
worrying that my mother—
in her one red cloth coat and
father in his camel hair blazer
and knit tie—would be beyond
any cry I'd raise there below
the courtyard and classrooms
and the monkey puzzle trees
twisting dark as seaweed
far into the air.
                    Home,
I climbed the avocado trees,
hung by my knees from a bough,
pennies falling from the pockets
of my jeans, confirming that
my place was on earth.
Coastal clouds strung out
like a Sumerian alphabet
and a crow was a riddle
of pitch and feathers against
the blue—I made no sense
of his clattering sound-bytes,
about how he saw it
all from there.
                    I came up
with no translation for the grey,
sky wide open for interpretation,
a polished page of longing
for which, I had faith,
there was resolution and
reward.
          Despite the blanks
I drew for the next 20 years,

I think nothing out of the ordinary
transpired—Assyrians continued
to descend upon the plain,
one fundamentalist after the next
ascended an orange crate
in the street to tell us
his God was God and what
all of us should do.
                    Oxcarts, barges,
horses, the refined blood of reptiles
from the Mesozoic era—we circle back
on ourselves with improved apparatus,
thinking we are going somewhere
this time alright, the fine print
about flesh and bones, barely
legible in the old provisos
the stars have always held
over our heads . . . .
                    What are the odds
there's someone behind the cosmic curtain
who reads our thoughts—a face peering out
bald and burnished as Ghiberti's
from his golden Gates of Paradise?
And I ask myself, Do I have time
to read about the Renaissance
again—what perspective is there
beyond the vanishing point
of the earth, the match stick anarchy
of light?
          Is anyone home
on Alpha Centauri, our nearest neighbor,
as our early TV waves arrive
with Howdy Doody and Flash Gordon
in his galvanized ship sparking away
in empty space as our first representatives,
with Groucho and his eyebrows,
the duck dropping from the ceiling
with the secret word?
                    How long
can we hold our breath as they check
100 million starry channels
at a time on the SETI dial?

Lucky, I guess, the NBC Nightly News
will be another 60 years
getting there, though our stealth
black-winged bombers are not all
that different from those in the '40s,
and the boys on all sides are always
blown to bits, their bones scattered
along the side of the road while
men in Savile Row suits step
into the bank.
                    Diogenes made his
homeless home in the streets of Athens,
ate his onions with contempt
for human achievement, and may have been
onto something, making a virtue
of extreme poverty. His only "challenge"
as administrators like to say,
was looking for an honest man,
holding that lantern for years in vain—
no grants, no pension fund—
you'd think he'd have caught on
at some point?
                    The blood-faced buzzards
spin up and glide beneath the strings
of evening without a mission statement,
but know what they are looking for,
feel it's fine to float there for nothing
more than the bequest of air.
                                        Down here,
our hummers are used to us
sitting beneath the extended arm
of our pine, the feeder suspended there,
as they lace their wire-like feet
confidently around the little perches
outside the flowery ports to glug
the red sweet water, but pause
to eye us up, still cautious
about creatures as statuesque
as we.
          Our cats learned long ago
not to bother about these birds
who burst through the air like particle waves

with feathers, and so they stretch out
for their siestas on the chaise lounge
awaiting their can of salmon
in fancy sauce served up promptly
at 5:00.
What's coming next
is anybody's guess, outside, of course,
the reliable collapse of our cells,
and how dispirited even the best
among us are about this one piece
of evidence we have, absolutely,
in hand. Nevertheless, I wouldn't
want to know right now, what
will become of me. Knowing that
you don't know is the best choice,
if, that is, you think you have a choice,
given whatever it is we are granted
a country mile short of illumination—
the limited-time gift of our ignorance
rising like spindrift, a savor of light
above the waves . . . .
At the end
of August, I'd be happy to know
we're finally going to get
some rain, happy with even
a small glass of local pinot
in the shade with which to salute
the incredible furnaces of the stars
that burn almost forever before
collapsing, exploding, and
gathering together again—atoms
whirling with their undisclosed
purpose toward the dark.

Cantata for Clouds and Bones

mis alas rotas en esquirlas de aire
—Jose Gorostiza

The wind was old,
the information of the dust
obvious—
neither told us anything.
The rain fell
through most of childhood
when the afternoon sun
wasn't trembling
briefly among the lilacs.
Rough angels,
their wing tips gnawed by desire,
stood in the stained edges
of light.
The evidence is
any three birds
lifting from phone lines
like half notes
rusting in the sky—
then the silent recitatives of stars. . . .
But it had little
to do with stars,
where we were formed,
where we will be
ground in fire
finer than the flour lost forever
in my grandmother's apron—
the grist of years
into almost
nothing . . . .

So I'll take any cloud,
a window still looking out
on a dream,
on the trees poorly dressed in November.
Then, I'll no longer
have to answer
to the stooges and big shots
who are running us
out of air,

and everything
will be blindness,
equal once again.

This cold
whistling by the window glass,
it feels like God
is sifting through my skin,
through the dulled phosphor
of my cells,
looking for his notes,
the elaborate schematics
of hope
he's sure
he placed there initially.
And when
everything inside me is grey
as a sheep's brain,
when he's done
with me for no reason
beyond cosmic grit
and gravity
draining away,
they'll make a small monument
from the available sticks,
and leave it
at the edge
of that childhood field
near the sun-bleached sycamore,
another place where
angels no longer patrol the rafters
of the sky—
one silence after another. . . .

Knife blade of the blue
for decades
at my throat,
the handkerchiefs of the 20th century
are drifting away,
surrendering
on the wind.
A shadow from a plane

blocks the sun
as if a hand
were reaching down
from heaven—
I say "as if" for none of us
are 8 years old
any more and believe
in the personal touch
of God.
I keep the moon
on my left
as I walk away,
my right hand across my heart
where I swear
to nothing.
There is no framework
for the light,
the spun threads
and loose trimmings
of the galaxies.
There are only fragments,
the splintered atoms
of my bones—
wings, if I ever had them—
floating
randomly on the air.

For the Saints

Rein n'y fait, menace ou priere
—Bizet, *Carmen*

Wind-swept
sea front, clouds
feathered into ellipses,
commas and
question marks,
long dashes
where the syntax
of life leaves off . . .

Fill your lungs,
the sky showing
its shelf wear—
that's it these days
for amazing grace,
the dress rehearsal
of everything,
the one psalm
your blood
aspires to.

But back up—
if only because
we were once young
and dumb enough
to throw down shots
of I. W. Harper
before finals
with our cursory
illuminations,
our synapses
breathing fire,
wearing away
a few grains of ignorance
to emerge none the worse
for wear.
Hell,
I walked home
from school every day

in re-soled shoes
when there was ice
on the poles, and
clean air in San Fernando
Valley, and according to
Sister Vincent de Paul,
St. Michael with
a flaming sword looking
over our shoulders.
I fell asleep in front
of Walter Cronkite
on the CBS news,
in front of Kitty Carlisle
and *To Tell The Truth,*
John Cameron Swayze
reminding us that
it keeps on ticking . . . .

This is no country—
as the old man said—
for old men. But it takes
one to know one—
the birds have flown.
You can stand here
as if your hair's on fire,
waving at the sun,
waiting to lift
into the sky
amid a shower
of mystic roses
like St. Theresa
but that will get you
nowhere fast. O
that still small voice
of calm is still so small—
we don our
parochial sombreros
but never ascend
to the beatified clouds.
And those clouds
you cherished all along,
they're not loopholes—

there's only one way
out . . . . the indigo night
batiked with stars,
hard-edged jumble
of imbedded clauses,
small print, illegible
in the margins,
which is a prerequisite
to the past,
to the next handful
of hendecasyllabics
in support of the war,
the same boys in the back
in pin-striped suits
making energy deals,
pay-offs, sending out
dividend checks from
Sanctified Oil.
                    Look,
the stars have been off-
kilter, up there
forever, trembling
relative to anything
you can put your finger on,
everything cooked up,
spun out on this mortal coil.
Beyond the cliff
you have the flicker
and burn of images
skipping in two-tones,
oxidizing in the replay
where you never were
a boy for very long . . . .

Most mornings,
it drives me to distraction—
the mist lifts off
the foothills,
and we all end up
with the same
sand in our shoes,
a psychic plaster

of Paris over the years.
You might as well
go on as if God loved you,
as if this planet were
breathing with you
one thin cloud
at a time, lightly as
the next cortege
of particles singing back
into the atomic mix,
the heavenly host
that may turn you up
again one day
on a beach—
4 years old among
the tide pools,
your parent's shell-
white station wagon
parked on Channel Drive,
almost no traffic on that
woodsy lane pushing
back the air . . . . Exhale
slowly now as the tide
slipping back after
each small wave.
Stretch. Your last breath
is out there, coming
to you out of the empty,
unmarked blue—
Wait for it . . . .

There's the aurora
borealis if you anticipate
transfigurations—
you can go blind
for nothing,
for any glittery get-up.
But there's nothing
like the cigarette girls
in Seville, chorusing
that *habanera,* the sashaying
passementerie of their

dresses, the bougainvillea
clicking with the castanets.
Carmen had an angle
on life, on love—
nothing helps, neither
threat nor prayer—
as if death were nothing,
as if you had all you needed
in the metaphysical bank.

We all know that
an angel—a red star
pinned above her ear
like a rose—will come
up behind us
on a side street
one evening, copper
light grazing her cheek
bone as she hands you
the briefcase, saying
she'll check around
back, reassuring you
that all the stardust
has been screened.
Remain calm,
there are no choices.
At the very least
we are all bagmen
for the saints.

Lead Penny: Early Lessons in Economics

One turned up in my change, a 1943 with wheat staves,
 a dead star among a constellation of coins,
half a century or so since the last one appeared—from The War,
 when copper was in demand for
shell casings—what any kid in the '40s or '50s called a "lead penny,"
 though they were steel, coated with zinc.
Most days, 1¢ was all I had to guarantee my participation
 in the high after school society
shouldering into the fountain, and while not near as flush as boys
 hauling down LOOKs, Abba-Zabbas,
and Milky Ways, I put my penny down and came away with
 2 red vines of licorice, and, back against
the star pine in front of the YMCA, spent my time waiting
 for the day to close above that tree
which was only a dozen steps below the clouds, my companions
 there on the edge of insolvency,
the iron-on knee patches of my school pants shining back at them.

The nuns were desperate to convince us that we should be
 storing up treasure in heaven
by fasting and making communion on nine First Fridays,
 days on which we had to finagle
money from our parents to subsidize the hot chocolate
 and donuts after mass. Donations
to the cafeteria coffers were compulsory, and bought our way—
 if you connected the dots—out
of hell fire and into the Starry Kingdom Club, where we would
 glad-hand the saints and everyone
who contributed to the party line and were contractually blessed
 walking those golden streets
of glory having placed their pledged envelopes of 1$ and 5$
 in the basket each Sunday.
I'd dribble in a couple pennies then, but brighter in memory
 is Tuck Schneider lugging
home a canvas bag after the Yankees won The Series again
 in September, each of us who bet
on the National League paying off our 25¢ in pennies,
 hoping his bag would break
and there'd be a scramble for the waterfall of coins . . . .

These bets cleaned us out
of discretionary funds for a month or more, which left
just Spelling and Arithmetic to fill
the vacant afternoons—hours wherein I calculated that there
were few rewards on earth, or
anywhere else, a problem that a coliseum full of theologians
could not begin to solve.
Death and damnation, we went through our lives bankrupt
of reason, one interpretation of iniquity
after another with the available outcomes hammered home
for 8 years of Catechism class
as we submitted our humble and coerced support, weighing
out an unlikely monetary salvation
against our modest investments in sanctifying grace,
our pockets empty as air.

But always, I want to take the world with me, worthless
nuts and bolts in an MJB can
still gleaming in motor oil, fragments and odd bits I was
blessed to have picked up
for nothing in the street, useless information, which
I unconsciously squirreled away
in class. 11 or 12, and I learned there was something
as bone-basic as cuneiform,
first writing like the arms of stars broken off and pressed
into clay. I knew the Hittites
had dibs on iron, and I could recite several sentences about
farmers in Latin. My father,
who could not begin to conjugate *amo, amas, amat*,
was sure I should, as it would
cement my investiture in the world of blue oxford shirts,
polished cottons, and penny loafers.
I would be brazed with the outward manifestations of,
and proclaim appropriate dictums
for, Private Enterprise, in a dead language for which
he'd paid plenty—but a buck
& a quarter and knowing all Gaul is divided into 3 parts
will get you coffee at *Denny's*.
After all the brilliant afternoons of autumn, it all adds up
to nothing. Yet, if I didn't know
better, I'd swear, looking out over the spindrift mists
of home, that I might just be
the one to survive it all, carrying that dull half dollar

of my soul with me in a lunch sack.
Half the time all I'm trying to do is sneak up behind
one of my memories and lift
some shiny object from a pocket. I would add the rain's
wish to my own—to fall
and rise again, surely as the grey currency of the sea.

Lying back on our thrift store couch, I'm reading
my 5,000th book of poetry, and so
have invested my time prodigally, so most market experts
would agree—no teacher now
to paste a gold or silver star on my white shirt collar
as reward for my reports . . .
I could have read home repair manuals, Taiwanese fusion
cook books, scientific self-help
best sellers, and so have been prosperous for myself or others.
But I'm an abstract thinker, mind
dense as coastal weather, clogged with any high or low pressure
system, thoughts as variable, scattered
and unquantifiable as a scrum of stratocumulus—ready with
a coin to flip or quantum particles
to split the difference with infinity. Short of that, all I have
are the books, a few rusted ribbons
of light tied around some left over parts with which I have
no idea what to do, and which,
all told, are no where near worth what they once were.

A Sentimental Education

> "I want to write the moral history of the men of my generation—
> or, more accurately, the history of their feelings.
> —Gustave Flaubert

A snowball's chance in hell
is what we had, that and hope
like a 50¢ piece in our pocket
we were dying to spend.
We stood brooding
in our skinny ties
and tab collar shirts,
staring down at our white socks
and polished loafers. . . .
This was a test, but not in Latin
or quadratic equations, this was
immediate social science
at the boarding school
where, as sophomores, we were
unprepared, pressed into the dark,
holding up the wall
for all that we were worth,
which didn't amount to much,
according to the girls bussed in
from the academies who looked away
each time one of us lost restraint
and risked the grand humiliation
of asking for a dance.
The gym
overflowed with heartache, yearning,
anxiety, and a dozen assorted
adolescent torments —the Shirelles' asked
"Will You Still Love Me Tomorrow,"
Barbara Lewis sighed "Hello Stranger,"
and, number one on the charts for weeks—
thumping intro down-beat, tambourines,
castanet's and violins—that wall of sound—
"Be My Baby" by the Ronettes,
driving us crazy, hormones like time bombs
pulsing in our blood, like barrels
ready to tumble over the lip
of Niagara Falls, every self-

conscious cell ready to burst
with the first sign of encouragement
which was miles from coming our way
despite the fact that each of us,
according to his natural gifts
and available materials,
brought to bear every scientific skill
we'd developed styling the wings
and waterfalls of our flat tops
and duck tales with Butch Wax,
Brylcreem, or Wildroot Cream-Oil—
high rolling waves as seen in photos
of Elvis, Fabian, or Fats Domino
on their album covers, the only clues
we were given to prepare ourselves—
inept and uninitiated as we were
for the longest of romantic shots.

Paul Anka's "I'm Just a Lonely Boy"
played, and the light flickered
off our plastered doo wop hair
and got us nowhere, observers
of that vast emotional under tow
just before us, as we did our sullen best
to adopt the casual manner
of an upper classman, who, staring
at the floor as if about to crush
a smoldering cigarette with his boot,
copied that surly James Dean glare
from *Rebel Without A Cause*
as if he understood the motivation
and reckless angst of '50s hot-rodders
who had no idea they'd soon become
the desperate insurance executives
and actuaries who parked their station wagons
in the carport each day after work.
The rest of us just tried to behave like
the rest of us, there being perhaps
one in twenty who could do the twist,
Hully-Gully, Mashed Potato or even
a rank imitation of The Surfer Stomp.
There was no way to arrive with experience,

none of us un-cool enough to face
our own reflection in the TV as we practiced
a new step at home while watching
American Bandstand.
                                        We were flying blind,
seat of our pants, life at arms' distance . . .
14, 15, and encouraged to socialize
by teachers in suits and stiff cocktail dresses
who were posted in every dim corner
ready to break up the older kids
lucky enough to embrace for 3 minutes
of mystery and minor electrical outage
as Kathy Young and the Innocents slurred
"A Thousand Stars."
                                        The likelihood of this
leading to happiness, knowledge, or especially
to anyone 1/5th as fabulous as Ronnie Spector
of the Ronnetts—or even to a trace element
of social grace or essential physical information—
was remote at best, not that we cared
in the least about the acquisition of manners,
cleaned up and going nowhere past
longing in the dark.
                                        I was years away
from a detailed understanding
of heartbreak sending me to the sea
on my motor bike to stare at the waves,
where it was all silence and sources
as yet unnamed, where I would be
oblivious to such luxury and good luck
as, looking back, it would reveal itself
to me forty years later—young,
plenty of time to kill, to indulge myself
writing some first melancholy lines
on a sheet of folded binder paper,
each image of anguish marshaled
within the light blue lines, each
precious misery it then seemed
would go on forever.

First Day of Retirement—Sitting in My Car at Miramar Beach During a Storm

> Science is a wonderful thing if one does not have to earn one's living at it.
>
> —Albert Einstein

I find it hard to believe
there's not some committee meeting
where I am due
to review the performance objectives
of something
as obvious as clouds,
hard to believe this is me
in the rear view mirror,
hair the color of clouds,
hard equally to believe
that somewhere
there are shining waters. . . .

Just up the tracks from here
I found Tuck Schneider
half-conscious on the roadside,
cheekbone crushed—
wheel locked up on his Honda as he crossed
the rails
50 years ago . . .
we had learner's permits
and motor bikes,
no helmets then, free
to ride aimlessly through our days.
I'd delayed a minute,
there in the little turn-around,
reaching out
a bit longer for something
limitless,
just beyond the waves . . . .
Invisible, of course,
our incontestable stars,
the shifts and dodging
reconfigurations
of fate—
all that speculation,
now so many
metaphysical smudges,
clouds of breath against the windshield glass. .

Nevertheless,
I am still here,
wasting more time with the sky,
the wind taking nothing
lightly.
My blood tastes of salt
and a little rust
where I've absent-mindedly bitten my cheek.
I've turned up a hundred
ways to express
my fear of death,
and placed them
amid the dazzling silk trees,
among the streetlights,
that same gauze and yellow glow
from Uncle Codge's
short wave radio
back there in the old country
of childhood
where I also recited Latin,
mastering the conjugations
of the vainglorious dead,
where the Hittites came up in Anatolia
with the initial public offering
for iron,
where Juvenal refined satire,
and thus political observation,
warning too late even then
of bread and circuses. . . .
I'm watching the gulls and terns
lift into the pearl-dull sky,
nonchalant, without a thread
of theory
to their names,
feeling, it would seem, that it's fine
to glide about
and look for nothing
for a time.
60-some years of guess work
and you'd think I'd have
an idea about what everything comes to?
There is no shortage
of supposition,
organized or otherwise. . . .
But I'm as baffled as anyone,
despite my devotion
to Albert Einstein—

first rate hero
of the working class,
who quit his dead boring job
in the patent office,
and thought for a living,
and so who was
never out of work.
Sockless and irreverent,
he was nonetheless determined
to interpret the fine print
and footnotes
of God's thoughts,
possessed as he was
of an empirical faith
in the imagination,
believing
there was something
ultimately there to be read. . . .
But he came up short
before the Grand Unified Field,
regretting
finally what they did
with the elegant distillation of light
and matter
he'd managed to decode.
Had he foreseen
the politics,
the fine grind of inhumanity
sewn into the atomic lining
of each
administrator's suit,
he would have turned sooner to playing
his violin alone in the kitchen,
turned to badminton in the back yard
with old pals to whom
he did not have to speak
English or explain
the elliptical transcendence
of a shuttlecock.
On this side,
or some other,
how empty our hands
finally seem to be.
Each evening, a few grey strings
tangle about
the leftovers
of the sea,

the shells and kelp,
such riches as I am left
to busy myself with
before the wind—
the daily indeterminate sands
revealing everything,
all there might be
about intention,
about the body
as a sustainable means
of transport for
a curious or industrious mind.
A last paragraph of dusk pads out
its sleeve-worn salutation,
pavement darkening,
black grease spots,
the ellipses of memory. . . .
Each moment in the universe,
burning away
as if it were nothing,
and we little more
than that for noticing
the related effects,
the chain link of light,
our impoverished gazing. . . .
Just a few humid layers of air
keep us
from the stars,
from a bright
relapse into dust . . .
the incomprehensible
everywhere
about us
like clouds,
stalled, then shuffling
aimlessly around,
looking
for something to do.

Schrodinger's Cat

In memoriam: Cecil B

Somewhere toward the end of my youth,
in that late '70s "finding myself" period, in that
semi-conscious frisson of gravity-defying body
and blood, I took a series of "development" classes
with a medium in Santa Barbara. Weekly
"hocus-pocus" as we called it back in the '50s,
going to Catholic school where we were
continually rounded up for funeral, high holy,
and First Friday masses—litanies, processions,
Stations of the Cross, bleeding saints, and Ascensions.
A little psychic phenomena then, was
hardly more far-fetched than everything
we'd been brain-washed to believe all those years.
So, as tables levitated and people's faces trans-
figured before my reasonably astonished eyes,
the paranormal seemed, by comparison,
more, well, normal.
Rev. George was an honest,
no tricks, nothing to sell spiritualist of the dark
room which blocked the daily traffic of our lives.
He'd gained celebrity working with Bishop James Pike
to contact his son "on the other side."
No gimmicks or gizmos, sessions came
at $5 an hour with a cup of tea
and some singing of old hymns. Two hours
which, if they accomplished nothing else,
calmed the mind's spinning core.
It turned out
I was adept at psychometry—the "reading"
of objects belonging to others, like the psychics
in old black & white films who help the police
find a kidnapped child by holding her shoe. . . .
I held a ring, or a watch, and a video
of a person's house—their life—ran in my mind
and I reported what I saw.
One evening,
George interrupted the proceedings to say
there were two small dogs, or perhaps cats,
circling in the dark aether of the room,
looking for me. Had I lost some pets recently?

No, I said. Then, they were awaiting me,
he said, a bit impatiently, at some point
in the future, that room of probabilities
always just down the hall.
                                        20+ years
would go by before 2 cats would enter my life,
and I'd find myself as unsettled about the afterlife
as the new science, the thought experiments
in quantum mechanics I half understood.
"Schrodinger's Cat" was one that threw
a wrench into the metaphysical gears.
His paradox intended to illustrate
that something can be in two places at once.
I flashed back to stories of Jesus in His 20s
recruiting among the Native Americans, and later
to swamis known to Paramahansa Yogananda
bi-locating in Banaras and Calcutta . . .
and that connected to Heisenberg's Uncertainty
Principle which demonstrated that you can't tell both
where something is and how fast it is moving,
and, that observation changes whatever you are
observing.
                In his mind, Schrodinger placed
a cat in a steel box with a vial of poison
that would break and kill the cat when
one isotope of a radioactive substance
connected to the box decayed and triggered it.
Schrodinger posited that the cat was in two
different states—since the observer cannot see
inside the box, the cat was both dead and alive
according to quantum thinking. But the question
remains whether the indeterminacy
of the sub-atomic domain transforms
into everyday events—cats vs. electrons—
dead or alive, and for 70 years everyone
has argued both ways.
                                        Einstein wrote
to Schrodinger that nobody really doubted
that the presence or absence of the cat
was independent of the act of observation—
something I'd pretty much worked out at 11
when I stopped believing we were going

to forfeit our place in heaven if we willfully
ate meat on a Friday . . . God and our guardian angels
were, we were assured, looking over our shoulders,
listening in and taking notes.
                                        Neils Bohr believed
that conscious observation caused events,
but also that if we do not look, there are no events,
just probabilities. The odds that those cats
would find me twenty years down the road
were, I'd estimate, about 2 million to one, times
a few billion particles pin-balling in the night.
I wasn't looking for Russian Blues,
they just presented themselves out of nowhere,
out of the chaotic salad of cosmic bits.
On a scientific level, it only seems a matter
of what you want to believe re. being
in two places at once, or anywhere at all
for very long vis-à-vis the observable
hard freight of the world, your basic
burger-and-fries realism, as opposed to
St. Catherine of Siena who took in nothing
but communion and light. For his part,
Schrodinger said later in life that he wished
he'd never met that cat!
                                        Is there someone
observing, causing events, or is what animates
our bones and sinew the result of a spin cycle
in the intergalactic wash? Atoms are decaying
from the get-go; neutrinos pass right through us
as if we weren't there, like the eyesight
of God (if meaning can be found
in metaphor), like the particle transmissions
when I closed my eyes in the classes
with Rev. George, and I saw what I saw.
The Aztecs wanted to know if there was time
somewhere else? My cats have no idea
they are going to die. Where are we
if we are not here, running around in the dark
for the time being, wondering if someone is
watching, if our lives can be saved?

Ontology by the Sea

In memory of Luis Omar Salinas

Aye! *vato*, *pistolero* of moonlight!
I know that's you,
there, beside the contingent palms,
in your grey agnostic shirt,
rolling up the long sleeves
of probable causes—
and not Immanuel Kant and the mystics
beachcombing at low tide,
tossing back the shells
of determinism
to the background
doo-wop of the waves.
No, it's you
in your existential pork-pie hat,
punctuating the air
with a cigarette,
marking your rhythms
with the spindrift
phenomenalism of the surf . . . .
Menthol KOOLS
as I recall—
you can smoke
all you like now,
no evidence remaining
of cause and effect,
hovering between
the salt spray
and spinning
atoms of desire,
between the lemon blossoms,
and the last Madonna
of Tenderness driving by—
your heart's wick burnt black
long ago,
no hint of an explanation why
the corporal works of mercy
never made it
to your front porch.
And when you remove
your hat to salute the sea,
it's still full of the ashes of romance,
the darkness in your eyes
envying the briny light
still breathing in mine.
And so I will not forget, *compadre*,

to take El Sueño Road to the shore,
to drive with the wind wings
open in the old Bel Air
a quart of Lucky Lager in the trunk,
for we still have much
philosophy to get through before
we find a foothold
in any realm, before we get out from under
the logical positivism of death
which we hoped to toss back
with the sea wrack and stinking kelp
to the committee
on the theory of theories.
You refused to sit for the examination
of the obscure,
to work out the long division
of the dark; rather,
you were off to climb balconies
with amorous offerings
to a sky that always remained
beyond reach.

About the soul,
you demonstrated as much faith
as the seagulls,
reciting their rosaries in the sky.
And I can't forget the dark angel
with a tight grip on our fates—
my back stiff now, rusted
like an old saw.
What was it
we found so empirical
in our hell-fired youth,
that made us sure
our lives were bound
to bloom
like the loquat sun over Mazatlan
where you arm wrestled
specters over the failures of rationalism
and instant coffee,
and across the backs
of bus tickets
wrote odes to the pragmatism
of sparrows,
notes for a paradigm
on the wristwatch of space,
the destiny of the universe
rising from the fires along the beach?
You sold your odes

to the professors,
refused to accept checks,
and gave to the less fortunate,
all the while still looking up
the skirt of misery;
and at designated points
along the way,
you took the bull
of madness by the horns
in *corridas* beneath
the cosmic sparkling abstractions.
We submitted
our metaphysical speculations,
our epistemological shoes
to the tide,
to the whirlwind,
the shattered ramparts of light,
and found ourselves
on the outskirts of Fresno,
1 a.m. in the Eagle Cafe,
lost among the galaxies
of grease.
All this way *amigo,* and it looks like
it's just air
to air
as your *compañero*, Neftali told us.
You've ascended
with the dust off the cliffs
to the sanctified levels
of the gulls.
And I'm over half way out to sea—
what banner should I hoist now
so God might see us
and know that we remain serious
and will not repent
the hundred anarchies of the heart
on this shore or that?
Here we are,
midnight above the breakers,
the sea still blank beyond
any helpful interpretation—
the sky, without one cloud
to run interference,
to speak
in our defense
against each false accusation in the stars.

Varieties of Religious Experience

> I am a deeply religious non-believer . . .
> This is a somewhat new kind of religion.
> —Albert Einstein

A mad scrum
of molecules
scrambling
into light
long before
someone breathed out
and thought
to ask
for reference,
require meaning,
expecting that
such silence
constituted the back-lit estuaries of our lives
and would lead
back, necessarily, to some initial sea.

Leaves in a whirlpool,
rain showers
across the fields,
an offering of smoke
against the grey
horizon's grid—
we worked up
theories
for our fears
maintaining, nonetheless,
that our past affects us
somehow in the future,
that the sky provides a context
and accounts
for me at 9 years old
in a world where everyone
sang along
with Perry Como on the radio
to "Papa Loves Mambo"—
#4 on the Billboard Chart—
as if things were ordered
for everyone to be happy.

It was New Year's day,
and again my father was
nowhere to be found.
I went along
with my mother and her friend Margo

to Butterfly Beach
where they popped a bottle of Le Domaine,
champagne
pink as the sunset sky,
and even I
was given a paper cup fizzing
with fading light . . .
and facing west
we celebrated nothing
as ponderous
as some predetermined
balance in the universe,
a scale model
metaphysical schematic
that applied locally to us,
but rather
raised our cups
to the last sparkling breath
of 1956—
the sea singing,
the seraphic salt choir of air echoing
in my unconscious blood
and purblind heart.

How to see a pattern now—
all the bent corners
and candle ends?
Last year my mother dying
in the dreary hospice
20 miles from her house
and I left her
for an hour or so each day
to feed her lonesome dog,
to take in the mail
when one afternoon
a roadrunner appeared
out of thin air,
out of the rocks and cactus,
came up onto the lawn, cocked his head
and looked at me
with the glistening dark star of his eye.
And I went up to him,
bequeathing bits of chicken
I'd cooked for the dog,
and the roadrunner
soon knew me
by my whistle,
by a sorry litany

of little clicks I made
and the sound of the garage door
ascending,
and he would wait under the oleander
for my daily offering.
I'd go back in and watch
for a minute or two
from the kitchen
window,
grateful for such radiant company—
the bright suggestion
of a soul—
who then disappeared
a day before
my mother died,
never to be seen again . . . .

Younger, I might have proclaimed
signs and wonders—
the wild green
parrots in the palms,
they must be
singing to someone . . . ?

And all the dazzling mathematics—
strings knotted in the invisible
dimensions of the cosmic wind—
don't they point to order?
But what is there finally
in the starry spectrum to persuade us
that the universe
takes a particular interest,
such inconclusive
prayers as the heart sends up,
so much dust pulled
from the empty
pockets of faith?
Beneath the coral and eucalyptus trees
the view is largely obscured,
yet I sit here
under the death sentence
of the stars,
each night holding
another breath,
as if
the escaping light
could be driven back
into the bones,
as if air. . . .

Time Travel

Sh-boom sh-boom Ya-da-da Da-da-da Da-da-da Da, sh-boom!

There are times, my mind in the clouds,
when I'd go back in a heartbeat. . . .
And, if that's how reincarnation works,
I'd return to do it all over again, even though
they say it's like repeating junior high—
outfitted for the '50s with a flat-top
and a clueless doo-wop consciousness,
pushing the buttons on the dashboard radio
between "Denise"—*Oh, can we kiss goodnight*—
and "Sherry"—*Can you come out tonight*?
Reduced to psychic essentials, such dogs
of innocence as we were.
God wasn't listening,
and the angels assigned to us took
weekends and summer vacations off,
the rules for this life and the next
having been spelled out in the handbooks
for numbskulls and non-abstract thinkers,
who were lining up in business suits,
skinny ties and tab collar shirts
for the sacraments and bake-sale coercion
fund raising for the church. Our TVs
were pitching prescriptions for ultimate
success in society, Bess Myerson
demonstrating the new Westinghouse
washer/dryer, the boat load of chrome
on a new De Soto.
Nuns required our reports
to be written with Schaeffer fountain pens,
and from their supply closet dispensed 5-pacs
of sky blue ink cartridges at 50¢ a pop,
much like the arrangements for sanctifying grace . . . .
How comfortable it all seemed—you wouldn't
want to examine things too closely
and lose your belief in Eisenhower
and eternal life, have doubts about
the station wagon starting up
when you turned the key.
More than anything

you want to be in love, to find yourself
in the blond arms of light at the dance
or parked 5 spaces back from her front porch
and the street lamp, your heart incandescent
as the filaments. . . .
                                        If you're at the sea,
you want to be surfing, with the invisible
photons shooting through the white foam,
not appraising the existential condition,
the ontological nonchalance of the waves
as a reference for hope, for any evidence
of call and response in the world. . . .

Back here, there's no point
in moving forward, in learning
the inevitable ten steps that lead to the fall
of the Roman Empire, the Incas, the British Empire,
or soon, the American empire outsourced
by the Chamber of Commerce to Mauritius,
the only known home of the Dodo
that quickly became extinct with European invasion,
Mauritius where there are no unions.
Robber Barons hired the Pinkertons,
the Black Water thugs, and who doesn't know who
handed off the concessions to Halliburton,
6-pacs of Diet Coke to GIs at $45 a shot—
pun intended—Black Water, black shirts,
blackhearts, with international headquarters
in the Cayman islands. Who doesn't know Franco
assassinated the poets of Spain, invited Hitler
to test-run his bombers on the Basques
limbering up for WWII while espousing Catholic
family values, fiscal belt-tightening?

TV on the fritz in my pied-`a-terre, so coming in
from work I turn on the radio and open
a diet ginger ale. The only station without static
has "easy listening" programming from the '50s
and I'm not sure what it says about my life now
that I immediately recognize Les Baxter
and his orchestra playing "The Poor People of Paris"
from 1956, or Frank Chacksfield's rendition
of "Ebb Tide?"

Both of which take me back
to our ranch house on Greenworth Place
among nasturtium, pittosporum and palms . . .
my mother in her striped pedal pushers
and auburn hair, leaning against
the half-open Dutch door. I am 9,
too young to know if she is lonely or content
as she sings along softly with The Modernaires
to "Perfidia." My father, off as always
who-knows-where, our Irish Setter thumping
his tale against the Frigidaire . . .
out on the patio, I've got my first transistor
in a hand sized leather case, repeating
nonsense with The Crew-Cuts to "Sh-Boom"—
Oh, Life could be A dream . . . . Then I'm back
in my condo, traffic noise rising
from the street, an original rendition
of Hoagy Carmichael playing "Stardust"—
everyone gone . . . the stars bright
through the sliding glass doors, the night
big enough to swallow all our dreams.

My Problems With Math, or Why I Don't Buy Lottery Tickets

I barely survived long division, the dividend, the divisor—
the 4th, the 5th grade? I was regularly separated from my funds
by friends at the candy store after school, no remainder.
In 8th, Sister Vincent de Paul thumped down Set Theory paperbacks
on our desks—numbers, letters, and Kabbalistic insignias
as the old figures still floated belly-up in my mind like a sea
of dead sardines. Only three kids caught on, two of whom
would choose accounting as the inspiration for their lives. . . .
The rest of us were threatened with the usual fire and brimstone,
VDP breathing flames and algebraic equations, steam rising from
her black habit as if hell were only inches beneath our feet.

In college, old Joe Buckley, the Christian Brother who taught
Trigonometry, might as well have been speaking Gaelic—
cosine, tangent, all that assorted nonsense about angles and spheres
was light years beyond the one-potato, two-potato arithmetic
at my command. He was an FBI—Foreign Born Irish—and passed me
with a D, pushing the limits of Christian charity for a young man
to whom he must have figured he had some ancestral ties.

Then, the Selective Service Test to keep our draft deferments
or run through the jungles near Khe Sanh, hot-footing it
past mortars, punji stakes, and bouncing betties, defending
the profit margins of Dutch Shell Oil, Colt Manufacturing,
the political capital of LBJ, Westmoreland, McNamara—
all of them knowing the score, cooking the books.
That test, given by the Educational Testing Service,
an organization with roots in the Spanish Inquisition,
was loaded with calculus, Trig, and multifarious equations.
I made as many blind guesses as they had 1-5 spaces to fill.
70 or above kept you off the next nonstop to Chu Lai,
and I scored 71? *SAPO*! as the boys on the east side said—
meaning, blind, unconscious, stupid, undeserved, rotten,
unmitigated, numb-skull Luck! I knew from nothing,
but came out a winner for once.

Until the Lottery in '69. Deep into a bottle of Gordon's Dry Gin,
my birth date was pulled # 318; above 245 wouldn't be called
the Selective Service agent told me when I'd applied for a CO.
I knew right then, as the rumpled old men in suits fished
numbers from the bowl, that I'd used up any luck I'd arrived with
on the planet. So later I didn't pitch in when colleagues pooled
money for scratchers, and even though Soto's brother won $10,000
buying a sandwich at 7-11, I never looked at the bright rolls of tickets
in liquor and convenience stores. I understood that no state grab bag
Lotto Power Ball Bingo was going to provide me with a lifetime
cash annuity, that OPRAH was never going to give me a new Chrysler
or an all expense paid Princess Cruise to Puerto Vallarta.

100 tons of dust hit the earth every day; NASAs funds have been cut
by congress so they no longer chart NEOs (Near Earth Objects)
the size of the Washington Monument or bigger, slinging themselves
in our direction across the hypotenuse of space. Minus a detection system,
will the odds of getting hit go up? You might make that bet, but the answer is
No, you just won't have as much advanced warning!

Einstein, without showing his work, worked out that God doesn't play dice
with the universe, which is an interesting integer of belief—
a non-statistical analyses, a wager which, if it's true, means the fix is in!
Even more reason, it would seem, not to push your luck.

Karmic hoopla aside, I had my horoscope read early on
and saw Saturn setting in my house of finance. Powerball's odds
of winning the big one are 195,249,054 to 1, whereas the odds of dying
from a meteorite striking the earth are 1 in 700,000. Even I can figure
it's more likely a decaying satellite or bit of space junk will take out my legs
than it is I'll win the Irish Sweepstakes. Each day it's 50/50 at best—
everything a factor of sub-atomic uncertain interstellar KENO.
I look around and think perhaps I should adopt the attitude
of that great philosopher Jimmy Stewart in *It's A Wonderful Life*,
realize I'm lucky to be alive, lucky that my grid of atoms took hold
in a California version of Bedford Falls and not Somalia, lucky

that I am not dying of any one of the variety of cancers on the menu
served up by the square root of chance to several of my friends.
I'm not taking any risks, not counting on any good fortune,
I'm tapped out. All I have left in my account is hope, hope's dust—
a belief in that longest of shots, that against every probability
my number will not soon turn up.

Nostalgia for the Infinite

> For after all what is man in nature? A nothing in relation to infinity, all in relation to nothing, a central point between nothing and all and infinitely far from understanding either. The ends of things and their beginnings are impregnably concealed from him in an impenetrable secret. He is equally incapable of seeing the nothingness out of which he was drawn and the infinite in which he is engulfed.
>
> —Blaise Pascal, *Pensées* # 72

> They will say all this is sad & instructive, but it isn't.
> Nor is there any scent of grief in such a story.
>
> —Larry Levis

Palm leaves like wings burning on the sea's sunrise arc,
        the star pine stepping off into air. . . .
The blanks are still blank and only the salt in your blood
        does not stand for something else.
Leave the newspaper on the walk, the daily crapshoot—
        a patch of sky still vague
where Larry and all the others skipped out on the threads
        of altocumulus, or where you recall
trivial faces from that '50s game show—Arlene Francis,
        Dorothy Kilgallen, Bennet Cerf, and
John Daly on *What's My Line?* No blindfold, no mystery
        guest signing in—just the usual old scraps
and grease spots, the unremedied past to work with. . . .

Everything considered—and these days you spend plenty of time,
        old sport, considering everything—
Pascal put his money on God, even though he thought
        he knew where we stand in relation
to infinity, in relation to nothing. Neruda confessed everything
        to the waves, to the salt air,
to his ghost-lit, sea-glass soul—associate saint of the spindrift
        shore. And Borges—eyes grey
as old moons, called even the houseflies to testify to the magical
        evolution of our shoulder blades.
Toss in Alberti naming each angel shaking out a few crumbs
        from eternity's tablecloth, the same ones
who have done nothing more than peek at us all along,
        and what do you have? Metaphysical
grab bag, last court of conceptual complaints, one that keeps
        no records of our appeals.

You settle for gazing out the window at that cloud drifting
over childhood's live-long day,
at children chalking stick men down the sidewalk who look,
old stick, more and more
like you—everything you promised yourself, just traces now
on the light diminished behind you.
Between here and there, the bushtits are diligent from buddleia
to the fennel, cleaning up
the boughs. It's Wednesday, sun riding out ahead of you,
seagulls dive-bombing the garbage
bags set on the curb—the world rotting every day, paying
no attention to what you do.

Then the Theory of Everything—each year a new interpretation
dances the *Merengue* down the halls
of science, across the glistening marimba of the Milky Way—
the dead stars just reaching us
with their back-ordered shipments of light. . . . You caught
the PBS series on WW II, though
you knew about the bodies in the tides at Anzio, Omaha Beach,
the thousands ground to pieces
for some General's two-star move to three, to the putting green.
You came in after The War—
those boys dying miserably under their bedeviled stars so you could
serve & volley, play 3rd, surf,
cruise in a '59 Chevrolet, and argue the irrelevance of Aristotle
when you were 20 and knew it all.
But isn't there more to that stamp-sized negative of your father
in his flight jacket? There's the glissandi
of electrons surrounding *String of Pearls*, *Moonlight Serenade*
as he stacks the disks, lights up
a Phillip Morris, smoke sashaying out the window above
the neon of the Rexall Drug.
Who remembers Yvonne de Carlo playing Lola Montez in the '50s,
and what about Dolores del Rio,
the sparkle from the screen dappling your shirt sleeves then?
Is there enough gas left in the tank,
amigo, to decipher the notes on Chaos Theory, enough for a foray

with the lost boys into the gears
and whirligigs, the innumerable jeweled movements of infinity?
An unlikely long shot at best. . . .

Yet you still feel you need to go to work, you're on your toes,
trying to land jabs and upper cuts
against the bobbing and weaving of fate, shadow-boxing
on your break with the indifferent
clouds—head down, guard up—spit the mouthpiece into
the motivational bucket. Truth is,
you've taken too many standing 8-counts and you're behind
on points. You've got objections,
direct them at the sky, watch them burst like confetti from a *piñata*
and trickle back down to you.

Your *compañeros* will understand if you hang it up, leave the vain-
glorious bones to every other
academic dog in line. Ice at both poles melting, your check
too late to save the polar bears.
Along the shores in Lompoc, grievances diminish with the rip
and undertow, with the pelicans
content in the orrery of wind. Forget the white roses that waves
will never wash into your arms,
allow the driftwood to set an example for adjusting to the world.
As a kid, you loved Swinburne,
sea-roll, and romantic roar—you were surfing when there were
still gods to be appeased.
Your buddy from Arizona died in Georgia, your pal in Pennsylvania
blindsided by heart as well.
And you even liked Bukowski, Bud twist-tops and all. Look,
no one was spared a hangnail,
let alone despair, bitterness, the usual slate of sad abstractions,
and you're sniveling over some
irregular beats? No one is saved. Say what you will, while
you can—the packet empties . . .
a little water, potassium, salt. So, a roll of the bones is all it's been,
and most evenings now,
wouldn't you let it all ride, double or nothing, for a decent cigar,
a glass of good red wine?

If we all prayed at the same time, what then? Sand jamming
the celestial works? I have my doubts.
I still can't differentiate lemon blossoms from stars floating
on the night air, the top down,
45 years ago on the sea cliff—something beyond the burning
atoms we share at random,
the cavalcade of molecules for as long as our individual particles
are lit and allow us to reminisce.
Song, 15 billion years of background radiation, gravity waves,
cosmic star gravel and interference,
theme and variation on desire, screech in the radio dishes, charcoal-blue
feathers of a Steller's Jay,
specific in the context of air, indeterminate against the void's rumbling
yowl in our blood. Insolvent instincts,
as if there were one chance in a trillion we would figure in the lost grid
of web-light—dust, replaced matter
the wind picks up as it interrogates the camphor trees that know
as much as we do about why
we've ended up at this point, our bones un-translated against space,
flanking the celestial dynamo,
nothing in the way of a clue but mumbling leaves. Isn't this where
a big imagination gets you?

For as much faith as you've put in History, for all the belief
Pascal wagered in favor of God,
and despite every scintilla of reason, we're still walking around
with a lot of dust in our cuffs,
debating with an immeasurable absence over things
we haven't received, or
those we have. . . . The wind, with all it forgets, moving through
cypresses along the cliff
is a good example— the birds stirring from their dreams as we're
looking at the distant lights winking out;
the sea isn't going anywhere. The Buddhist scholar would accept
the choices available and be calm
as pebbles on the bottom of a stream, he'd raise a cup of rice wine
to the twilight, to absent friends,
and for the time being, watch the heavens expand, drift,
and be forgotten where they fall.

Islands Moving Beneath Clouds

> We like to be out in nature because
> It has no opinion about us.
> —Nietzche
>
> Metaphysics is a consequence of not feeling very well . . .
> —Ernesto Cardinal
>
> When I do not walk in the clouds I walk as though I were lost.
> —Antonio Porchia

From high on the mesa,
the sea bends down,
then rises to the horizon,
rounding off
where a barge rides eye-level with the sky,
floating
up channel
past Santa Cruz and Santa Rosa,
toward San Miguel—the islands
sliding beneath
a sun-splintered terrace of clouds. . . .
I feel the slipstream
from the outlines of space,
the fanfare of the wind as it inflates
my jacket,
as if gravity had doubled
inside me
like sand filling a bag . . .
my breath
sifting into mists,
into ellipses of doubt. . . .
It's all gone by so quickly
I have to think
it surely couldn't have mattered
all that much. . . .

Head in the clouds,
the highlight reels go by,
little parings of eternity . . .
white doilies
on the couch and arm chairs,
tables in a parlor where
they're drawing cards
from a thinning pile—
a place as grey

as Washington Court House, Ohio,
where my father was raised,
where I visited
my grandparents and Aunt Veleska,
the low atmosphere
dim as skim milk. . . .
I had my own outlook
on the tracing paper sky,
lonely in the company of fair-weather clouds.
No reason to look beyond
the pirate galleons,
fish bones, vertebrae, ribs of a wren,
the Himalayas
of the air. . . .
Thunderheads rose
and thoughts of Jesus did not
come to mind,
though the Book of Acts had him elevated
in a cloud,
the Virgin likewise taken up.
In medieval times
God was a hand or eye
emerging from a cloud,
but I saw elephants parading
trunk to tail,
or the sagacious face of Albert Einstein.
Ancient Hindus
said cumulus were the spiritual cousins
of elephants—
and in Sanskrit,
at the beginning of time,
elephants were white, had wings to fly,
could change shape
to bring rain.
In school,
during rainy-day sessions,
clouds drifted past
the high transoms of the air—
mostly, it seems,
in black and white,
like the opening for Paramount films,
the mountain
floating on a lake of clouds,
the stars circling,
spinning in from space. . .

I no longer believe
God hides
in back of the clouds.
I sit on the beach
with a small driftwood fire
and watch the fog ease in
like the cold blossom
of time,
tight-lipped as ever about its intentions,
about the white ash of light
rising,
calming
the delirium of the sea.
My blood tastes of the waves,
and barely holds back
the undertow, the underlying
guesswork,
the essential salt that,
like God,
allows us to hope,
to see a light glimmering
beyond that place in the road where
we stopped to think about the stars
shining all this time
for nothing.
Our new lemon tree is flowering
like a spiral galaxy, yet I'd settle for
the insubstantial,
a glimpse
at the underlying schematics
of the wrist watch
on God's arm. . . .

To get where we thought we were going
it appeared we had to leave
home, travel to capitals, inner cities,
next stop before
the back of beyond—
minor novelists,
copy editors, assistant vice chairs
of the ad hoc committee
on misery,
meeting on the mezzanine
in our starched white shirts,
our second-hand tweeds. . . .
And all we were ever after
were the green

reassurances of youth—
ball field, corner grocery,
Drive-In,
the last soda fountain. . . .
Good times, death beds, and heavy songs,
as my *compadre* Omar
inscribed his last book
by way of farewell. . . .
Coming up on 65,
I rarely sit up late
with old revolutionary associates,
drinking bad wine and castigating the dead-
boring,
the one-book wonders—
gone, that great empty joy
we could once afford,
happiness for an hour
despite the pressure
building in the arteries,
the tipsy electronics
or skipping rhythms.
Who wants to be content,
to sit breathing,
admiring the dust particles
suspended on the light,
watching stratocumulus,
drumming
our fingers on the arm of the folding chair
to keep time
with any bit
that's left us here?

I watch The Bear Flag
blowing in an off-shore breeze,
can see time
moving there . . .
the sweet anguish of childhood
as I tugged my cap down
against the cold, waiting
for my parents
to collect me before dark—
or of adolescence,
whole afternoons spent
sitting in the sun's stream
of consciousness. . . .
But here I am,
with the scuffling surface

of the sea,
the overcast,
the practical and imminent
matriculation of dust,
and no going back.
I never saw myself
here in the outer provinces
of lawn chairs and un-raked leaves,
looking for the black-throated
Grey or Hermit warblers
passing through,
a cloud of them sliding down
the sky toward warmth. . . .
Those winters
down town after school,
everything was always so far away—
clouds white as cotton swabs,
in the high wide windows
of Woolworth's,
headed out the left hand corner
of the blue
promises of faith.
What harm could it do now
to pardon
the fading allegiance
of our stars,
the spindrift story
of the sea,
to go
where clouds eventually go
when they're gone. . . .

Personal & Metaphysical Derivatives

sus huesos yacen
caidos en el povo
—Eugenio Montejo

At 5, I picked up French with ease
attending a parochial school
my parents couldn't really afford—
le morceau de gateau!
I knew a table from a window,
the book on the desk from the stars
in the sky—*le livre sur le bureau*
de l'école a patri des etoiles
dans le ceil, voila!
I was almost sure of things.

30 years later, in Paris,
I'd held onto just enough
to know not to order *tete de veau*
from the menu, to be able
to ask for *un demi-kilo*
fromage des Chaumes
at the market, spending
my first meager grant money,
convinced I was investing
in the future.
As I understand it
now, we are conglomerates
of small strings more invisible
than air, than light . . . even
the leftover parts of stars,
everything there is on this side
of the dark, or some other
parallel side—all that
is finally nothing you can hold
in your hands. . . .
We have only
the immediate consignment
of clouds to fill the afternoons,

to subsidize our speculations—
and yes, I was an over-serious kid,
pulling my white pant's pockets
inside-out, turning my palms
up to the sky, to show
they were empty
as those very clouds . . .
I waited outside the store
while others dispensed with
their discretionary income—
allowances, or pocket change
filched from the bureau-top
in their parent's bedroom—on
Mars Bars or Milky Ways.
                                        But
those were short-term dividends
and soon we'd race our bikes back home
to fish sticks and Franco American
Spaghetti or Spam and canned peas;
this was, after all, near the bottom
drawer of the lower middle class
who spent their income dressing up
as entrepreneurs, a word my father
invested with specific moral gravity
as he inserted staves into the collars
of his starched shirts.
                                    We had,
as models, members of The Junior
Chamber of Commerce, John Foster Dulles
who refused to shake the hand
of Zhou Enlai, Eisenhower, and Nixon
in their bad suits, playing golf,
cutting deals to sustain
General Motors.
                              No one talked
about Korea or the deficit anymore —
there was just a short intermission
before Vietnam. In passing,
Ike mentioned the Military
Industrial Complex on his way

to retirement and the first tee
at the Club, waving from the back seat
of his Eldorado.
                                        On our porch
above the creek, I held talks
with my white tom cat, TJ,
and we listened to the wild peacocks
register their objections
from the oaks . . . it was the '50s
and we were the last ones still
running free in the foothills.
In earlier socio-political quarters,
Johannes Kepler and Tycho Brahe
were just making trouble
as they worked out the laws
of planetary motion
while they played cribbage
each evening beneath the peg board
of the stars. I later saw it
as a toss up between
Spinoza and Pascal—
God is the free cause of all things,
or, the flip side, Atheism is not
a good wager. Your odds set
against the ontological clock
ticking in the middle
of nowhere with no hedge fund
to back up your bets.
                                        In Prague,
The Communist Museum is right
between McDonalds and the casino.
Now my childhood house in our seaside town
seems further away than the haphazard
and residential stars . . . for instance
ARP 273 in the constellation Andromeda
300 million light years from earth;
what looks like a perfect merger
in the shape of a rose is actually
two galaxies connected by
a thin bridge of stars, 10s

of 1,000s of light years apart?
Go figure how long until
the pay-off?
                    When our bones
lie fallen in the dust, what remains
of you or me is at best
some recycled light,
some depreciated chemicals.
For now, guns or butter,
metaphysical puts and options?
The account balance of the sky
still looks empty. My poor cat,
Cecil B, died a year ago this
August—his last days on earth,
or only all his days on earth. . . .
What can I take away from that?

Back Room at the Philosophers' Club

> Dear philosophers, I get sad when I think.
> —Charles Simic

Each evening, before I step through
the grey door, before I hand off my
moth-bitten coat and hat, I stop and look up—
all the purchase I am ever likely to have
on hope. . . .
                I then calculate
with a glass of dry port, gaze out
into the obscured clockwork of stars
where I am usually dismayed
as I again consider the frayed cuffs
of fate, the whirling of the wheel,
the weary subject of appearances,
and whether life evens out?
                                        At best,
my math is bad, but the numbers
obtain—over the last 50 years
more species have gone extinct
than during the preceding 4 billion.
In America, more people were
killed by guns between 1979
and 1997 than died in all
its foreign wars.
                        What are we
thinking? I no longer bother to ask
what the boys in the back room
are having, no doubt an existential
martini or two, dry as the '50s . . . .
And on the subject of an afterlife
I was fed no more flimflam
and folk tales than the next one,
and though I had my doubts, I threw in
willingly enough with the rest
for a while . . . .
                        Fridays in college,
we played 7-card-no-peak, betting blind,
passing the penny-ante hours,

the bottle of *Early Times*,
the 6-pack of *Lucky Lager*,
ignoring questions of eternity
as if we'd never heard
of Immanuel Kant and the Mystics
though we all yelled "Everybody Mambo"
as soon as the first notes of Xavier Cugat
came through the wall
of the Cuban student's room
next door.
Since then
I've been doubling down
as if we were nothing
in the sight of angels,
as if all this time I'd not been
rolling the bones in the dark,
wearing down the chances
that my number won't come up—
betting on a crooked wheel because
it's the only wheel in town,
knowing the odds are stacked
for the house, deducing that the dark
takes it all. . . .
The leaves outside
the window cut the starlight
to pieces, and, if you buy into
phenomenalism, your memory,
for the time being, seems
as easily unquestionable . . . . There is no
secret in the ocean air that edges
into night, that leaks past a horizon
that went grey as ash two hours ago . . .
the sea, soul-blue, deep
as a bone-bruise, rakes in your last
metaphysical chip. . . .
Our atmosphere
eats away at our skin, cosmic grit
and after-effects of light, scraping
down, to ectoplasmic particulate,
to conjecture. . . .

Whichever
way you figure it, we cash in
our loses each morning as
crows sit high in the civic oaks
examining our discards, inured
to the loss of lemon groves
the parking lot obliteration
of the air . . . .
Corporate dealing
from the bottom of the deck—
no one's surprised the sea is burning,
white flames in wind. What can you get
for a new hypotheses, all of us
headed alone together
into the great phylum of dust
and quantum debris? The stars
offer the same melancholy
rondos,
nothing's changed much
since the Baroque, since explorers
arrived in little boats to cart off everything
they could from the natives
in the name of Christ and King.
You play,
of course, the hand you're dealt—
you need to profitably occupy your time,
improve your mind,
though the cards are marked,
though the rain closed all the roads
in front of you, and the shoals of clouds
stuttered with every bit
of historical indifference
imaginable. . . .
Nevertheless, for now
you're here, examining a hand
of well-reasoned inferences,
breathing away for whatever
you reason you're worth—
just out the window
those scuffed clouds

are apparently impartial,
content enough to wait
and wager on what might
take our place here
as we think things over,
everything, that is, that will,
in all probability, outlast us. . . .

El Cielo

Adentro de la luz
circula tu alma
aminorandose hasta que se extingue

—Neruda

I have an understanding with the sky—
each day I attend
the capitulation of the waves back into the blue
and don't complain
too much . . . we look less and less like ourselves,
though it's still us inside.
Youth gone, the knotted string of middle age, all up
in the air like laundry
in a breeze, until we barely see ourselves disappearing
in the swirl of dusk.
The closer I come to the sky, the more I want to believe
this is not it—
that I'm still headed somewhere, anywhere at all. . . .

In the park overlooking the sea, I sit beneath
coral and eucalyptus trees
and breathe deeply alongside the crows—it's free,
and the company, though ruffled,
is reliable, all of us bemused, looking into the aimless sky. . . .
I set my bag down
and pour a cup of pinot noir, first sip as balanced as
the blue evening humming
out there above the island's edge. A second taste
almost transcendental
as I send my *saludos* to the clouds where I hedge my bets
that it's just the evening mist
shifting up there, and not the angels who've overlooked
their assignments here.
Tomorrow, I'll take another stab at making some sense
of this . . . but in any case,
caramba, it was fun as it flashed by. Might as well
put more red poppies
and geraniums on the balcony and cheer the air up a bit.

No fall, no winter here—shirtsleeves whipped in a Santa Ana
            10 months out of 12
it seems, and like the trees, I'm a bit unsteady, exposed
            here on the cliff
in one of my dozen Hawaiian shirts picked up at the thrifts—
            all cotton, old school,
surfers on long boards at Diamond Head, sail fish in the air,
            hibiscus flowers and coconut palms
swaying in that 60's light still fading at the ocean's edge. . . .

            Hernandez warned us
about the tree of impossible things, and though I believed him
            I still climbed branch
by branch as high as I could. I read philosophy in my 20s
            and came to see that
I didn't have much to say, but wanted to say it anyway.
            And though I've never
imagined my heart as an orange, or a burning pomegranate,
            there still might be something
to the soul layered like an onion, that dust cloud sifting down. . . .
            I'm out here working now
every day to unpuzzle the mockingbird's oratorio to life,
            the *coplas* of spice finches
congratulating each other at the feeder as they hang on
            in the off shore breeze. . . .
The froth of breakers along the shore catches me out
            in the damp air that
nevertheless saves me from the stars, from our imminent
            relapse into dust
glimmering above the sea, where not one prayer has kept
            those birds in the air.

(for good Pablo)

The cypress take their shapes from the wind, grow old,
            and like our minds
sketch a poetics of absence. Yet in the leaf-green
            and lacy shade
of pepper trees, I think of you maestro, *compañero*,
            and call you back
from the solar mists, from the winds blowing toward

the empty rooms
of eternity. Step out from the ribs and arm bones
of your odes,
say death means less than the undertow
murmuring in the tide,
singing for nothing in our blood. Give us a *grito*
or two to chase
the *politicos* over the cliff, a song to repair the back ache,
the stitch in the side,
numbness in the leg. Give us a trail of sea foam,
crusts of sunlight
leading beyond the white caps that reveal the irony
of every wasted appeal.
No one is fooled when we lose one comrade after another,
when every breeze
miscalculates the sorrow of abandoned sidewalks,
the death of rose canes.
If we praise our shoes, or the two tomato plants
we raise each spring,
if we proclaim a dishtowel the happy flag of our republic,
even these scraps
of joy blow away through the blue leaves of evening
as the light goes out
across the shore, inside of which the soul spins
down and is gone . . .
the air-sealed kiss of salt in spindrift lost above the sea.

Walking Around

Yo paseo con calma, con ojos, con zapatos,
con furia, con olvido
—Neruda

When I get to the corner
the street lamp's still broken,
black wires hanging up there
like the entrails of a star.
When I wet my finger
and hold it up—the forecast is
for dust, more dust any day
you choose. . . .
                    I get out early,
arm in arm with the shadows
before they dissolve
into thin air, heat
ascending the bluffs.
If there's a sliver or two
of cloud above the horizon,
above the inexhaustible
solitude I sometimes share
with the sea,
it's just a little punctuation
on the blank sheet of the blue,
some starred complaints
on the wind's inscrutable list,
a little nagging
from our fate that's
not about to change.

Some mornings
a heavy fog pulls
on my shoulder bones,
my hamstrings singing
out each time I bend
to admire the day lilies.
It's no use wondering
where the time has gone,
or the lilacs, the loquats,
the yellow blossoms
on the tipuana trees—

as far as metaphysics
are concerned, there's only
that itch at the back of my neck,
the spindrift tossed up
from the rocks,
the backdrop of what
still looks like oblivion
from here.
                    Downtown,
restaurants crowd the sidewalks
with little iron tables and chairs
for tourists to be seen eating
their salads. It's difficult
not to bump my knee
or slip to the curb as I pass,
my brain still trying
to account for the old
store fronts—the news agent's
selling El Productos, Dutch Masters,
the used book shop,
its musty caverns,
drilling light through shafts
of dust and time . . .
on the corners, Silverwoods,
Woolworths, Montgomery Wards. . . .

Once I thought
I saw my father at the
cracked Formica counter
in that tiny coffee shop
on Carrillo, and I still see
my mother standing
on State Street, in front
of the displays at Lou Rose,
window shopping for nothing
she can afford. . . .

The air's stretched thin
from the silted windowsills
to the shore, to some point
on the horizon where
I just can't see

any further. . . .
I want to shout
to the bus driver,
the panhandlers,
the passersby—STOP,
I've had it up to here
with everyone forgetting!
But I stroll on sensibly
down the street
like a retired building inspector
still looking for cracks
and water stains—
recalling what I can
before the bits and pieces
of memory's ladder crumble
and the light burns up
with the useless supplications
of the leaves, the dust of space,
the spokes of the stars,
the near or far intervals
of silence everything slips
away to. . . .
                    I'll get there
when I get there—
I want to take my time
if I still have any, and if
there's a moment to spare,
who knows where it is?
I'm just shuffling along
in my old coat and shoes,
nothing in my arms,
not even the fanfare of birds,
all which make me
finally even with the sky. . . .

Reincarnation by the Sea

> The whole day isn't enough anymore
> To live for half an hour.
> —Julio Cortazar
>
> *Mi deber es vivir, morir, vivir*
> —Neruda

If I woke up now back in the black & white '50s,
the wind parsed in Latin
through the false acacia, a background laugh-track despite
Sartre and the existentialists
there twenty years before us smoking *Gauloises*
and drinking *Pernod*
in cafes as if they too were going to live forever—
and all the old TV props
in place, the pitcher of milk on the kitchen table,
gingham tablecloth,
cereal boxes of *Post Toasties* and *Nabisco Shredded Wheat*—
would I believe
I was anywhere at all and thank my lucky stars
with an orchestra playing
Isn't it Romantic, the champagne popping, Audrey Hepburn
walking onto the terrace
in her diamonds and black gown? Even in1964, my last year
in high school, my girl friend and I
watching *ZORBA THE GREEK*, there was Alan Bates
looking like an insurance salesman,
and me looking like Bates—thick dark hair, closely cut,
white starched shirt
of an irresolute man of letters—or so it was for his character,
and the life I thought
I might one day turn up. He'd come to the island to run a mine,
but was going crazy
among his books for no reason I could figure out
but which my girlfriend
whispered to me: he was in love with the raven-haired widow
and could not decide
to go to her. When he did, he was too late and outnumbered
by the ignorant knives
of the fishermen who killed her. At 17, I knew from nothing,
was oceans away from Zorba,
who buckled his pants up and just sailed off after life on a whim. . . .

Lead-colored clouds,
pale leaves drifting above the shore, how far back
do you want to go—
old dreams, that hazy brilliance of childhood when time
always took too long?
Plato had us in a queue in the sky, sliding down
like a saline drip
through the ionosphere . . . and our Bible History book
informed us that Constantine
whacked boatloads in the sign of Christ, sent them packing,
metaphysically speaking,
at the Milvian Bridge. So even if souls are recycled,
there's no accounting
for the current increase planet-wide? If the math means anything,
ever truly adds up,
where did all the new souls come from—there were far fewer
of us ten centuries ago?

Now, just the dust of afternoon blowing up from the road,
the billion particles
that are all that will likely become of us, overcomes me . . .
a grey, sandy light draining
from the world, just above where the foothills had gone
up in ash the summer before,
where the seabirds disappeared in clouds, the green
water songless before me.
I coasted on my bike—no hands—down the middle of the road,
against the invisible
arms of the wind working slowly against me and what I knew
would likely come.

Attached by memory, I see them line up still—Schneider,
Fowler, Carlson, Knapp,
Ortegon, Armour, and Sozzi, spacing themselves evenly
at arm's distance
in front of the classrooms before the Pledge of Allegiance
and Salute to the Cross.
And it takes little to guess what's waiting for them—poverty, war,

or, if lucky enough to side-step
one form of corporate conscription or another, they grow—
according to their talents
and grab-bag portions of luck—old in what's been called
the fullness of time,
that pinch of dust in your pants' cuffs that you started with.
For my part, I've strung images
together like stars cut from newspaper, or folded, threaded,
and hung to yellow in the sun.

Once, I expected the heavens to confirm or deny the substance
of our substance, to override
crop circles, animal gods, one god who, rolling the bones,
threw boxcars and came up
with the Big Bang, cause and effect that covers it all—
who left some order
for every sub-atomic particle and bit blown forth in the redshift
of creation, who sets everything
in motion, everything happening because of anything that
any one of us did before.
If that is the case, where is the French Laundry on Milpas Street
run by the Chinese family
who sent their mute prayers and starched clouds of steam
heavenward 6 days a week
and who put the bluing in my father's dress shirts,
the staves in his collars
so he could formally do business, who returned our sheets
and towels bundled in blue
paper and tied precisely with a string as if the world
were just that ordered?
Somewhere, I kept a pair of my father's cufflinks in case
I ever picked up a shirt
in the thrift with French cuffs—keeping tabs on time. . . .
That's why most mornings
I can't forget Bing's improvised lyrics for "I Can't Get Started,"
realizing I haven't finished
even half of my work: "I dig the 4th dimension, but I get
no attention from you."

A banker writes 9 bad poems and no one pays attention;
        a poet writes 1 bad check
and it follows him his whole life. Anymore, I rarely stay up
        with comrades from my 20s
reciting the old poems, the impromptu manifestos, tossing cups
        of sparkling vitriol
over our shoulders for luck or in memory of Bukowski, because,
        in the long run,
the results proved useless despite an immediate purgative effect.
        Old river, broken boat
of moonlight, we row closer to sleep, drifting toward everything
        they say now lacks
substance and light, any stop-over point for consciousness.
        While our chemical value
has increased over the last decade, our minds might be
        only the aggregate
of those chemicals, self-referential as the implosion of a star.

        A wave then, a packet,
the adumbrated seed of that always tangential light
        shoots by, only a flicker
of images you once filtered through the crepuscular gauze
        of your mind repeating
or reconfigured—no ghosted oxidation or reply in your bones. . . .
        The life you chose,
if you think you ever had a choice, good as long as you loved it.
        So you love every
thoughtlessness scraped bare from the sky, each temporary
        membrane escaping
your hands as you wait in the dark for reruns, instant replays,
        to take your place.

All those years floating on a raft of error and
        ambivalence, a great
empty joy beneath me, half of everything I touched
        unintended . . . I began
to favor trees over pastoral philosophy, and driving
        the freeways it was
obvious that we couldn't all sing along with the infinite
        nor recognize its tag line

when we heard it, no more so than the ticking half-life
of any atom or steadily dimming
element carried within or without us slip-streaming
through our veins,
through the gravel and corpuscles of space. Some nights,
the choir of coyotes
on the mesa, seem to intuit as much of our predicament
as there is to know.
Moon or no moon, lives change, and who ever gets it
right the first time?

For 50 years I've sat down with the sea, with myself and tried
to arrange my thoughts,
a chain of figures cut out of paper that leave me with nothing
I can put my finger on,
though I've never mistaken the wind for the touch
of the dearly departed,
or for the wing-brush of an angel, despite the semi-mystical
and assorted misfortunes
suffered at Catholic school. What was revealed as the glory
of man in texts and institutions
did not appraise well when compared with the sun-colored
fruit of the loquat,
with kickball diamonds cut by our feet into the playing fields
of spring. Absence of evidence
is not evidence of absence. I keep going back and forth—
another stage, an alternate
layover traveling outside of time and our cosmic back yard?

The prize no doubt goes
to entropy as we drift absent-mindedly as clouds through
the world until we reach
a point where no one was expecting us—60 something
and no going back,
exiled to a province of bones with the distant ringing
of the sea in our marrow. . . .
It was always far away, that moment inside time
exactly divisible by itself,
waiting in the high uncalculated blue, floating
diacritically above

our heads, invisible in the sempiternal molecules
trafficking an oxygen, nitrogen,
and argon infusion inside our veins until the body refuses
to pay out any longer,
until the lens at the edge of night through which we view
the lost blossoms
of the universe goes on adapting with or without us—
a fifteen-billion year
addlepated rumba of fates in the roseate gas-smear
and dot-matrix of galaxies,
one chaotic proposition of oceanic membranes, in all
probability, like another,
where they may or may not give all the pasts and
futures another spin. . . .

Cloud Memoir

boys perish while you go upstairs
to write your memoirs . . .
—Adam Zagajewski

Speak softly: you're no longer young—
the sky never lets you out of its sight . . .
on the horizon, clouds remind you
of the Sisters of the Poor, then the everlasting
flames—the thin gauze of belief which does little
to obscure one beggar proclaiming
to another, shouting over a feast of flies.

Arriving after the 2nd War, rinsed in the grit,
in the grey ash and aftermath of winds,
we should not forget who saved us,
even for a world that rose in billboards
and skyscrapers, measured and shining in no time
from their blood.
No one is immortal—
that much is clear . . . otherwise, it's all
mythopoeic hodge-podge, metaphysical
mix and match right up to this afternoon
where a shoal of clouds stretches until it fully
represents an ichthyosaur—the long snout
and short-armed fins abandoned by time,
the fish-boned beast you saw in your 6th grade
science text, a book which did nothing
to explain to you or anyone where it went?
Whatever the dream, it's over with
before you know it . . . in your old jacket,
a 1,000 Lire note and ticket from the vaporetto,
crumpled beneath the crush of memory.

Who gave it all up and moved to Paris,
to a five-floor walk-up eye-level with the grey,
who figured it out despite the barking dogs
peeing on copies of *Le Monde* spread out
on the kitchen floors, despite the underworld
rumbling of the *Metro*? All that head-in-the-clouds

was fine so long as you had the Francs for Beaujolais
and baguettes. You stayed home, sat at your desk,
but in the end our memoirs prove nothing
against our atoms unscrambled to the stars. . . .

Your soul at a standstill—neutrinos passing
unnoticed through your cells for no purpose
whatsoever. At the bottom of things,
the infinitesimal mechanics and disorder
of the world above which you arrange
your post cards of Santorini and Menorca,
the brown & white snaps of your mother
as a girl on the farm—it's not as if you had nothing
left to do but fly to Vienna for a coffee, as if
you could profitably spend a rainy morning
listening to glum Wagner's *Twilight of the Gods*
a second time.
                    Puccini's another matter—
the notes of *La Rodine* like swallows' winging
in the evening, *chi il bel sogno di doretta* drifting
out the brown doors of a café in Piazza Navona
where you have enough finally to drink
a *Fernet-Branca* at your leisure in the late afternoon,
a cinnamon-colored light, October sifting down,
the singed leaves of the plane trees yellow
across the *campo.*
                    Surrounded on all sides
by such regrets, what are you going to do?
$10 gets you another *Fernet-Branca*, a bit more
time to digest the past, which turns you out
on Divisadero, at the Eagle Café, 1 AM and Omar
covers his fried eggs with his hat just to see if
anything will change when he lifts it up,
the unemployed psychologist studying
the owl-eyed souls on their solemn stools
to predict who's off their meds, who'd be the first
to dial up Kierkegaard on the pay phone, or who,
18¢ short on the check for the Blue Plate Special
will confront the cook with dialectical materialism—
a place where it was always no dice 'til dawn
all along the bar to the bus stop.

You were 30, nothing
hurt for long there on Arthur Street half your life ago;
the rooms large and cheap, the sorrowful zoo two blocks away,
peacocks pleading for mercy each morning . . . the light was free
all day and with your *compadres* you said whatever
you felt like it to the sky, did your editing on the late shift
at the Basque Hotel.
Ten years earlier, you escaped
the war and ran the streets in your waffle-tread Nikes.
You held court beneath the apricot recalling Xerxes
and Westmoreland, anchored in aluminum lawn chairs
as twigs burnt in the BBQ where your fates were unreadable
in the smoke, in the confusion of coals and stars.

Someone opened a bottle of Carignane
so we could praise ourselves in our obscurity,
praise the Phoenicians who brought the vines to Italy,
half-blessed as we were with a little history that kept us
from an office and investments in mutual funds.
There was no dispute over the mortadella and
cracker bread, over the sweet butter and hard biscuits.
The light sank, the first star rose above the tips of cigarettes
that glowed and spread with the constellations.
You did not talk politics, or quote bits of Latin,
though you were covered with the ancient dust
of both for any good it might do. You listened to Bizet
instead of Mahler, imagining cigarette girls sashaying
to the *habanera* across the living room, someone balancing
on one foot, wine glass held high, everyone chorusing
"Car-moon . . .", mice in the walls waltzing on their toes. . . .

Like drifting cumulus, dark rungs of history
dog-paddled across the hills where Nietzsche
dreamed of fame, where instead of studying
our philosophy, we sat around a card table
playing Black Mariah, 7-card-night-time, Jacks Back
to Lowball for nickels and dimes, for anything
we were worth.
What that eventually got us
was seats on the board of The Institution of Weariness
which, at 5:00, has you on the patio, content to watch

a rank of humming birds scramble to the free-drink feeders
hung on the eaves, the penny-dreadful clouds slipping in
from the indifferent sea, where the dead forget us
the way a liquidambar lets go its leaves,
the way those clouds churn eastward, regroup
and reappear darker over a city as grey as Minsk.

The liquidambars wave in the wind, and not much
is disclosed against the blue, immobile there
as if entirely innocent of our prodigal dispositions . . .
no alibi, no supporting witnesses, just a few
wisps of cirrus overhead to remind us that,
we're no better than those who paid too much
attention to philosophy, and who, looking to the sky,
missed most of the goings-on.
The dust that lifts off
the leaves like so many prayers that saved no one, went up
to the stratocumulus stopped out over the sea,
where the sky is white, where, no matter what you think
the clouds say, there's no more stalling for time.